SCHOOL
OF THE SPIRIT

SCHOOL
OF THE SPIRIT

Operating
Powerfully
in the
Spirit Realm

ROBERTS
LIARDON

CREATION
HOUSE
BOOKS ABOUT SPIRIT-LED LIVING
ORLANDO, FLORIDA

Copyright © 1994 by Roberts Liardon
All rights reserved
Printed in the United States of America
Library of Congress Catalog Card Number: 93-74610
International Standard Book Number: 0-88419-360-8

Creation House
Strang Communications Company
600 Rinehart Road
Lake Mary, FL 32746
Fax: (407) 869-6051

Dedicated to the 1994 Spirit Life Bible College charter class graduates:

Max Charles Achey
Marc Amino
Tracey Amino
Kerry Dean Anderholm
Linda Elise Anderholm
Lorraine Ruth Bachtold
Carol Brown Bagley
Ann L. Bandini
Drue Allison Bingham
Gene Bivens
Robert Paul Burbatt
Michael Lee Cantrell
Christian Lee Carroll
Suzanne Marie Carroll
Kathryn Ruth Gansow Cherif
Hyonhwa Chong
Laura Lynn Clint
Simon D'Arcy
Paul Davis
Furman Delgado
Michelle Delgado
Robert Michael Dodd
Belinda Jane Dover
Diahann Joyce Ducran
Cheryl Lynne Dunham
Derek John Dunn
Charles Edmonson
Melinda Faith
Patricia Lee Fisher
Richard Ivan Fisher
Carmel E. Garcia
Jerry M. Garcia
Bill Gibson
Sherry Gibson
Loretta Greer
Vladimir Gutsman
Gordon Harrison
Pearlene Harrison
Benjamin J. Hegenbarth
Rolph Randolph Hendriks
Catharina Hermansson
Randall Scott Hix

James Raymond Hoffman
Jayme Horton
Walter A. Huezo
Rena Lou Huntington
Steven Michael Huntington
Dorothy Marie Jeffrey
Derek J. Johnson
Ronald G. Judge
Sharon R. Judge
Day Sung Kang
Jason King
Daryl Lawson
Diana K. Lindsey
Kurt R. Lindsey
Margaret M. McGushin
Melody Ann McPherson
Troy Marshall
Lloyd Vinson May
Kenneth Wayne Moore
Larry Gerome Moore Jr.
Amy S. Muranko
Kirk Newallo
Donna Jeanne Nordquist
Marcelyn Lei Norris
Elizabeth Tayo Onilude
Donna O'Reilly
Lorrie Kathryne Owen
Eva Gail Peterson
John Andrew Ram
Linda Lee Ram
Hosea Ramdeen
Mary Hannah Regan
Tammy Marie Ricks
Mickela Denee Slocum
Cynthia Joan Smalley
Andrea Sobrien
Sandra Karen Sweet
Patricia R. Thomas
Hendrik Van der Merwe
Randal W. Wiebe
Kathryn Anne Wing
Dorothy L. Wright

CONTENTS

THE BELL IS RINGING

As a kid in school, you knew instinctively something that most grown-ups in the body of Christ have forgotten: If you didn't make it to class, you would miss something. Sure, you may not have liked it. Perhaps you only attended school every day because your parents made you go and the law said you had to. But still you understood deep down inside that the lessons, the homework assignments, *the training,* were good for you.

Over the past few decades, a laziness has crept into

the church. Conditioned by our quick-fix, drive-thru, gotta-have-it-now culture, we have come to expect instant everything in the Christian life. We whine that we've tried to live the victorious life, but it's just too hard. It's too much work.

We've even convinced ourselves that any type of spiritual labor is "striving." So we sit back, sending up halfhearted prayers and waiting for the miraculous to zap us into the supernatural kind of life Jesus said His followers would lead.

> And these signs shall follow them that believe; In my name shall they cast out devils; they shall speak with new tongues; they shall take up serpents; and if they drink any deadly thing, it shall not hurt them; they shall lay hands on the sick, and they shall recover (Mark 16:17-18).

What was it that distinguished these New Testament believers from their Old Testament counterparts? Both groups feared God; both obeyed His commands. Yet something very special was given to the New Testament believers that Abraham, Isaac and Jacob never dreamed possible. The very Spirit of God — what Jesus called "the promise of the Father" — came to dwell within them.

No wonder the early Christians "turned the world upside down." The power of God was resident within them! The divine force that spoke the world into existence now indwelled their spirits.

Back-to-School Days

Over the past several years I have come to realize that the church needs to go back to school. Not grammar school and the three Rs, but what I call the school of the Spirit. So strong was this impression that in 1992 I felt led to open a Bible school called Spirit Life Bible College in Costa Mesa, California, where my ministry is based.

The contents of this book are based in part on the curriculum taught at Spirit Life Bible College.

My Schoolmarm in the Faith

Everybody needs a mentor, and for me that person was my grandmother. From the time I was five years old she helped train me in the things of God. Grandma was my spiritual schoolteacher — the one who drilled the lessons into me and saw to it I never cheated.

Her training mostly involved prayer and reading the Word. She encouraged me to pray as much as I could — pushing me past my comfort zone to build endurance in prayer. She made me eat the Word until it became a part of me, until walking in the Spirit was a way of life that I would never depart from.

That's what I hope this book will do for you.

Each of the chapters in School of the Spirit can be considered lessons in your spiritual training, but the real-life results depend on you. Lessons won't do you any good unless they are acted on.

Jesus, Our Headmaster

Jesus never intended for His followers to live weak, wimpy, powerless lives. His Word tells us clearly how to walk in the Spirit and be led by the Spirit on a daily basis. Yet I am convinced the majority of Christians lead substandard spiritual lives. They rely on their senses and feelings more than the Spirit's leading, often making decisions as critical as the choice of their mate on the basis of how they "feel."

Church, wake up! God desires that you be more than conquerors, not groveling children who are knocked down by every wind that blows. There is so much more of God available to you if you will only reach out and take hold of Him, if you will appropriate the clear teaching of His Word.

Jesus, our headmaster in the school of the Spirit, is ringing the bell, calling all who desire more of Him to come and learn. Will you take the challenge?

ONE

YOUR ARK OF SAFETY

Open your Bible to page 1, and you will find four of the most profound words in all of Scripture: "In the beginning God..." (Gen. 1:1).

All things begin with God. All things have their origin in Him. Sometimes our minds cannot fathom this fact. But we can know it and be confident in it, for the Word says it.

Everything you face as you learn to walk in the Spirit will begin with God. You cannot start your education in the school of the Spirit without meeting Him.

A lot of people try to begin the life in the Spirit by meeting someone who knows how to activate spiritual laws. But if that person doesn't live a life of holiness — if he doesn't live for God — then his disciples can wind up just as corrupt as he is, full of devils or even dead. Life in the Spirit is serious business, and you'd better be prepared to treat it that way.

The realm of the Spirit does not begin with an experience — it begins on your knees with a decision to go on with God. If you desire to live a successful life, your starting point must be God.

Created to Commune

Genesis 1-5 records the story of the creation of the world and the human race. The Bible says that God created Adam out of the dust of the ground. He breathed life into him and caused him to come alive. Next he fashioned Eve. God blessed Adam and Eve and gave them dominion over the whole earth. He created them to commune with Him and to take care of the garden.

They were told by God not to eat the fruit of a certain tree, but Eve, being deceived, did. And Adam, following after, ate of the fruit also. In this one act of indulgence they lost their position in the Spirit.

When Adam fell, he did not just lose something natural; he lost a spiritual level he had been created to occupy. The Bible says that Adam and God walked together in the cool of the day. Man lived in a state of spiritual revival before the fall. He lived in what I call the move of the Spirit.

Adam and God walked and talked every day.

Heaven and earth were in complete harmony. There was great fellowship between them. God would come down and talk with His creation. He loved man. He wanted to be with man. And man began to learn about God and what God did.

But man sinned and was kicked out of the garden. However, in Genesis 5 we read about another man named Enoch who proved — after the fall — that life in the Spirit was possible. He was so in tune with the Spirit of God that he never actually died. He just left earth to go be with God. That's talking and walking in the Spirit!

Genesis 5:22-24 reads: "Enoch walked with God after he begat Methuselah three hundred years....And all the days of Enoch were three hundred sixty and five years: and Enoch walked with God: and he was not; for God took him."

Two other people have always stood out in my mind as examples of walking with God. One of them is Noah, whom we can read about in Genesis 6. The third man who modeled Spirit-led living is Abraham. These three men — Enoch, Noah and Abraham — lived and walked in the Spirit under the old covenant. They didn't have the benefits of Christ and the new covenant. They didn't have the spiritual benefits we have today. All they had was faith. But they knew life in the Spirit was available.

Through their examples, others learned how to operate in the glory and spread the news that mankind could still walk with God. But now it would cost more.

A Price to Pay

Because of Christ, we have it a bit easier than those

in the Old Testament. But there is still a price to pay. That price is obedience. Life in the Spirit doesn't come on a silver platter, my friend. It comes because you are willing to pay the price night and day, night and day. And you have to keep on going. Your life has to be one of continual growth.

Life in the Spirit begins with obedience to God. I cannot overstate how important obedience is in order to maintain your life in the Spirit. A life of continual obedience will carry you to new levels and depths of the Spirit.

A lot of people want to get way out there in the realm of the Spirit, but you can't get out there until you understand this point. The decision to enroll in the school of the Spirit really comes down to a choice. When you choose to walk with God, that alerts Him that someone has made a step toward Him. But if you wait for God to come to you, you might be disappointed for a long while because He doesn't know if you want Him. You have to tell Him you want Him.

God is polite, not rude. He doesn't barge into your home. He doesn't barge into your life. He comes and presents Himself, and you either accept Him or reject Him. You either receive what He says or reject it.

God wants every person to live in the Spirit. No, I'm not just talking about being a Christian, but living your life in a new realm where natural laws are superseded by spiritual laws, where you can walk and talk with God as Adam did before the fall.

You have to prove to God that you are serious about walking with Him. God isn't going to come down and show you the mysteries of His kingdom if He is not sure you are going to live for Him tomorrow.

He's not foolish. A lot of us think we can fool God, but remember that He's God!

One reason why people don't maintain their lives in the Spirit is because they have no reverential fear and respect for God. They look at Him as a great big Santa Claus in the sky. They read His Word, but when it shows them how they should change, they don't obey it.

To live in the world of the Spirit you have to be ready for constant change. You have to learn to be secure in change. If you fight change you won't go far. The Bible says we change from glory to glory. And the glories don't stop even when you get to heaven. They just continue. Paul told the church at Corinth: "But we all, with open face beholding as in a glass the glory of the Lord, are changed into the same image from glory to glory, even as by the Spirit of the Lord" (2 Cor. 3:18).

The Sin Barrier

In order to maintain your life in the Spirit, you have to understand that sin does not pay. Spiritual things cannot go hand in hand with sin. Sin and glory do not mix. When sin and glory collide, it causes a spiritual reaction that produces judgment or death — which is what happened to Ananias and Sapphira in the book of Acts.

This couple thought they could fool God. They sold a possession and brought the proceeds to the apostles, but they kept back a portion for themselves. Peter, anointed by the Holy Ghost, perceived that Ananias and Sapphira had tried to deceive the Holy Spirit. They were struck dead on the spot and had to be carried out of the church.

You can never hide sin from God. Because He's omniscient and omnipresent, He knows and sees everything. I don't say this to scare you but to warn you.

Some people are more scared of what people might say than what God might do. I'm more scared of what God might do than what people might say. Words aren't as powerful as the acts of God. When God begins to deal with you about sin, He doesn't form a committee to discuss the issue. He tells you, "Change or else," because He's God.

Some people think that God is mean, that He's going to "get them." But that's not the character of God. God does not break people, He heals them. He binds up their broken hearts and releases them into new life and new victory.

God's not against you. He may convict you of your sins; He may bring reproof to your life and rebuke what needs to be rebuked. But He always does it in love for the sake of bringing forth good fruit in your life.

You Can't Manufacture It

When I started in the ministry as a teenager, I thought everyone lived in the Spirit. I thought everyone lived the way we lived in our home, because Grandma and Mother told me that this was the Christian life. I thought every family that was Christian lived the same way. I found out we were one of the very few.

Why are there so many lukewarm people today?

Why are so many people having problems in their lives? Why, when you hear messages about living in the Spirit, do you get upset and think you can never get there? It's because you're lopsided. You only see the blessing. You don't consider the price of sin. You see, sin has a price too — a high price. When you know what can happen if you choose to walk in disobedience, it will help keep you on the right track.

You can't fool God, people. You might fool a man and say, "Yes, I'm in the Spirit," but you can't fool God. You can't manufacture the real thing. You can't manufacture true spirituality.

Your first requirement with God is to maintain your life with Him. Get your life straight with God and continue an everyday process of growth with Him. If you're not growing in the Spirit, you're sliding backward. There is no neutral ground. You are always going up or down in the world of the Spirit.

But living in the Spirit doesn't come simply because you are real sweet. It doesn't come just because you smile and look nice on Sunday mornings. It doesn't come because you give thousands of dollars to a church. It comes because you pay the price of obedience every day of your life. It comes because you choose to obey God even behind closed doors.

God wants you to be a Christian every day. He wants you to be just as real when no one is watching. He desires for you to pray in tongues, fight the devil and shout victory when no one is there to say, "Man, you're spiritual!"

Spirit life is a command — not a suggestion. The earth is heading for the greatest tribulation it has ever seen. The Bible warns us of it. But there is a way out.

God always makes a way of escape for the righteous — just as He did in the days of Noah.

The Ark of Safety

Noah lived in a similar society as we do, surrounded by evil men who willingly chose sin over righteousness. Yet Noah stood out among the crowd. He chose life. He chose obedience. He chose God. And God provided a way of escape from the impending flood. The ark was his safety.

As the ark was to Noah, so is Spirit life to the believer today. God gave Noah instructions on how to build the ark, and we have instructions on how to build a productive life for Christ in these end times.

The ark was a protective habitation that God instructed Noah to build to preserve his life and the lives of his family members. God promised to protect Noah and his family from destruction. But notice that Noah had to do his part. He had to be obedient and get out his tools and go to work. The ark didn't build itself, nor was it hand-delivered, prefabricated by God. No, the ark required effort on the part of Noah.

God has made a way of escape — a way of safety — for us too. That way of safety is life in the Spirit: confronting every situation from the stance of the Holy Spirit within you and coming out on top of every situation. But, like Noah, we must follow God's instructions if we are to build our "ark" properly.

Noah told the people of his day that the ark was their future. It was their destiny. If they didn't get in, they wouldn't have a destiny. They would die. The people laughed at him.

Their jeers didn't faze Noah. He kept building the ark until one day God told him to get in it. Noah called to the people once again, "Come and get in! This is your last chance! It's your last hope!"

Just as Noah called out in desperation to the people of his day, I'm calling to you, to anyone who will listen. It's time to get in the ark. It's time to get serious with God and begin to walk in the Spirit.

TWO

BUILDING A
STRONG SPIRIT

Our God is strength. He is not weak, nor does He value weakness. God wants us to be strong and mighty *in Him*. To walk in the Spirit, we must develop spiritual strength.

Listen to what God told Abraham in Genesis 17:1:

> And when Abram was ninety years old and nine, the Lord appeared to Abram, and said unto him, I am the almighty God; walk before me, and be thou perfect.

God didn't say, "Crawl before Me, and be halfway perfect." No, He said, "Walk before me, and be thou perfect." So this idea that God is weak, God is wimpy, is a religious thing. Religion loves you to be ignorant and weak. But God loves strength. God's nature is strong.

David wrote: "Who is this King of glory? The Lord strong and mighty" (Ps. 24:8).

We need a revelation of God's might and strength. If He lives in us, then the power that raised Christ from the dead can be activated in our lives. To live below what God has given us in our inheritance is to be disrespectful of Him. To not take of the provision He has made possible for us is to be disrespectful of Him. To not receive healing when it's available is to be disrespectful to the stripes He bore.

Why Spiritual Strength?

There are two sources of strength for the Christian: the human spirit and the anointing of the Holy Spirit. Most people prefer the anointing because it's like a gift. But your spirit is just as important. You have to learn to live strong without the anointing. You have to learn to do what's right without the outward anointing. A strong spirit is not a gift; it's something you have to discipline yourself to build.

Great men and women never fall because of their anointing. It is their weakness of human spirit that makes them do the shameful things that we later read about in the paper.

What is spiritual strength? Why do I have to be strong? Why do I have to train my human spirit? Why can't I be a nice Christian who just sings "Amazing

Grace" and goes to church and loves the Lord the way I want to?

To answer those questions, let's contrast the lives of two men who were both anointed by God but whose life stories had radically different endings. Why? Because one man developed his spirit and the other did very little of that.

Destined for Greatness

Joseph and Samson started their lives in very much the same way. Both were called of God, both were anointed of God, and both were known of God.

Genesis 37 and 39 tell the story of how Joseph was brought down to Egypt. As a young man, and his father's favorite son, he dreamed that he and his brothers were binding sheaves in the field, and his sheaf stood upright, while his brothers' sheaves bowed down to it. When he told his eleven brothers about the dream, "they hated him yet the more for his dream, and for his words" (Gen. 37:8).

Then Joseph had another prophetic dream. In it the sun, the moon and eleven stars bowed down to him, which symbolized his father, his mother and his brothers making obeisance to him. He told this dream to his brothers also.

Already they despised him because he was their father's favorite. But this second dream was the icing on the cake. The brothers decided to get rid of Joseph once and for all — or so they thought.

Do yourself a favor. When you have a dream, keep it to yourself. Or tell it to someone who can handle it.

Joseph learned maturity the hard way.

His brothers threw him into a pit but then decided to sell him to a caravan of merchants on their way to Egypt. And so Joseph was brought down to Egypt and sold by the merchants to Potiphar, an officer of Pharaoh and the captain of the guard.

Genesis 39:2-3 reads:

> And the Lord was with Joseph, and he was a prosperous man; and he was in the house of his master the Egyptian. And his master [Potiphar] saw that the Lord was with him, and that the Lord made all that he did to prosper in his hand. And Joseph found grace in his sight, and he served him: and he made him overseer over his house, and all that he had he put into his hand.

Potiphar made Joseph the overseer of his house, and God blessed the Egyptian for Joseph's sake. Verse 6 says Potiphar "left all that he had in Joseph's hand; ...save the bread which he did eat." He trusted Joseph so much with his possessions that he didn't even know what he had. "And Joseph was a goodly person, and well favoured" (v. 6b).

I've been with some preachers who, when they are under the anointing, are so sweet and wonderful you just want to hug them. But when that anointing lifts, they act like a grizzly bear who's been shot but not killed. They're angry; they're greedy. That's probably the grossest thing I've ever seen in my life. They come out of this glorious anointing, and greed and anger hit them.

This happens because they have not built the right

character, the right human spirit. When there's a weak human spirit and a strong anointing, you have a schizophrenic life. You have Dr. Jekyll and Mr. Hyde. That's not the will of God for us.

If you work and get your spirit to be as strong or stronger than your anointing, your life will be an example to others. Like Joseph, you will be well favored. But if your human spirit keeps getting weaker, your life will get more and more bizarre.

When Potiphar's wife asked Joseph to sleep with her, he refused. That's proof of a strong spirit inside Joseph.

Now let's look at Samson.

Power Gone Wrong

Samson had a magnificent life from the start. An angel appeared to his mother and told her not to eat or drink any unclean thing while she was pregnant. The Holy Spirit came on him when he was a child. His problems started when he refused to marry a girl from among the tribes of Israel. Instead, he chose a Philistine woman for his wife. He married outside the will of God, and that's when his trouble began.

We know the story about Samson. Judges 16:1 says, "Then went Samson to Gaza, and saw there an harlot, and went in unto her." That all happened in one verse. At least Joseph had several verses to get to his refusal. Samson accepted in one. Samson went down to Gaza, saw a harlot and said yes all in one verse. He had little spiritual strength.

Samson's story continues in verses 2-6:

And it was told the Gazites, saying, Samson is come hither. And they compassed him in, and laid wait for him all night in the gate of the city, and were quiet all the night, saying, In the morning, when it is day, we shall kill him.

And Samson lay till midnight, and arose at midnight, and took the doors of the gate of the city, and the two posts, and went away with them, bar and all, and put them upon his shoulders, and carried them up to the top of an hill that is before Hebron.

And it came to pass afterward, that he loved a woman in the valley of Sorek, whose name was Delilah. And the lords of the Philistines came up unto her, and said unto her, Entice him, and see wherein his great strength lieth, and by what means we may prevail against him, that we may bind him to afflict him: and we will give thee every one of us eleven hundred pieces of silver.

And Delilah said to Samson, Tell me, I pray thee, wherein thy great strength lieth, and wherewith thou mightest be bound to afflict thee.

Three times Samson played a joke on Delilah.

And Delilah said unto Samson, Behold, thou hast mocked me, and told me lies.

And it came to pass, when she pressed him daily with her words, and urged him, so that his soul was vexed unto death; that he told her all his heart (Judg. 16:10,16-17).

Joseph's Choice

If we compare Samson and Joseph, the one we could understand for making a mistake would be Joseph — not Samson.

Joseph was raised by his father to be a good Israelite. He was reared to have concern for the things of God. The Lord talked to him in dreams. But his brothers were jealous of him and sold him as a slave. Now what if that happened to you? It's easy to read this story in Genesis as a story, but somebody actually lived it — this was his life. This involved years of his life.

So here is a young man who was sold into slavery in a foreign country. Can you imagine how he felt? Once he was a free man favored by his father, and now he is a slave to an Egyptian.

He could be angry. He could say, "What's the use of keeping the laws of the God of my father? He's done nothing for me. Look where I am. I'm a slave in a foreign country where they don't even know His name. My own brothers sold me!"

You can see in the natural that if one of these two should have made a mistake, it should have been Joseph. But Joseph wasn't the one who made the mistake.

It was Samson who had the militant power, Samson who was a one-man army, Samson who had the great anointing. Yet he couldn't take care of one woman.

Let's go back and look at what happened to Joseph. It is so similar.

And it came to pass after these things, that his master's wife cast her eyes upon Joseph; and she said, Lie with me.

But he refused, and said unto his master's wife, Behold, my master [has given me everything] in the house, and he hath committed all that he hath to my hand; there is none greater in this house than I; neither hath he kept back any thing from me but thee, because thou art his wife: how then can I do this great wickedness, and sin against God? (Gen. 39:7-9).

Your physical body, when it wants sex, doesn't recognize covenants. It doesn't see the wedding ring — it only knows desire. That's why when you wake up in the morning after your body has been satisfied, and your conscience kicks in, that's when the regrets start. Your body has no conscience — it just has wants. Remember that.

Your conscience is made up of your spirit and your soul. It understands covenants, laws, commitments and morality. Joseph had developed his spirit to the point that it kept him from choosing sin over righteousness.

He said to Potiphar's wife, "Your husband has given me everything but you, and there is an obvious reason why we shouldn't do this."

To me this is phenomenal. Here is a young man who was sold by his brothers, enslaved in a foreign country, yet who still kept to the covenant of his God. He had something built up on the inside that gave him the ability to realize God had control of his life. His spiritual strength gave him the ability to say to Potiphar's wife, "No! That would be breaking the covenant with my master, and breaking an even greater one with my God."

Then look what happened — she lied. Joseph was thrown in jail. Now he had another reason to be angry. He was served unjustly. Not only that, but everybody forgot about him. He was left there to rot.

What gave Joseph the ability to continue following God even with all the tragedies he faced in his life? What gave him the ability to say no to Potiphar's wife and keep his covenant with God and man?

Samson was not in jail. Samson was not taken captive. Samson was out playing. He had the greater anointing. Joseph might have been wise, but Samson had raw, brute, anointed strength. But he went down to Gaza, fell in love with a woman and was tricked by her. He couldn't resist her. He couldn't say no. The first time she said, "Tell me where your strength is," he should have stormed out of the house and made a hole in the wall on his way out.

But no. Big on the outside, wimpy on the inside — big anointing, little spirit. Anointing does not resist the devil. Anointing does not break temptation. Anointing will not help you at that point. You have to have something on the inside of you to do that.

If everything depended on the anointing, then none of this would have happened to Samson. Two verses, and Delilah would have been dead. End of story. But the story does go on. Finally she discovers the secret of his strength. She tells the Philistines, and they cut his hair and prepare to capture him.

> And she said, The Philistines be upon thee, Samson. And he awoke out of his sleep, and said, I will go out as at other times before, and shake myself (Judg. 16:20).

He did not know that the Spirit had departed from him. It's a sad day when men and women wake up and find that part of their life has come to an end.

> But the Philistines took him, and put out his eyes, and brought him down to Gaza, and bound him with fetters of brass; and he did grind in the prison house (v. 21).

If you don't build a strong spirit, you will lose the ability to see or discern, you will lose your liberty, and you will end up doing another man's labor.

Passing the Test

I have presented these two stories for a purpose. Joseph was sold as a slave by his brothers and ended up being a type of the Savior by saving his brethren from starvation.

What if he had slept with Potiphar's wife? They all would have died. The story would have a different ending. But Joseph did what was right. He kept to the law of his God and didn't let the trauma of his soul or the enticement of his flesh pull him into sin. He had strength to hold the reins of his being.

Why do you need to be strong? 1) To control your flesh, 2) to keep your soul in line and 3) for obedience to the high call of God on your life.

How do you build a strong spirit? How do you become a Joseph and not a Samson? I spent almost the whole chapter making this case clear. Now I want to give you answers.

First let me restate that it's not the anointing. Charismatics and Pentecostals are the world's worst for always wanting a new anointing. Thank God we can get the anointing, but we live by the development of our spirit. God is not going to send an angel out of heaven or give you an anointing to take care of your personal life. He will undergird you and strengthen you and help you. But He expects you to do what you know to do.

Your strength is not measured by your anointing. Your strength is measured by how you live your life; that's your gauge.

Why are there so few greats, as we call them? Because men and women don't take the time to become like Joseph. They settle for being Samsons. They like the quick rise, the *oohs* and *aahs* of flattery, the fame and fortune. And often they lose it in one night.

The steps to building a strong spirit are twofold and amazingly simplistic. But if you do these two things, you will build a strong spirit in your inner man.

- "Eat" the Word of God.

You develop a strong spirit by putting the words of a strong God into your being. But notice I said *you* put His Word there. It doesn't happen automatically. Whatever degree you go into the Word will be the degree that the Word provides you with strength and understanding. If you go in shallow, you will have shallowness. If you go in deep, you will have depth and strength.

Some people read the Bible just to find out what they can get. Thank God for His blessings and promises, but there are also verses that correct us and give us right understanding. I call them *correct me* verses. There are the *bless me* verses, and there are the *correct me* verses. You need both in your life. If all you do is live in the *bless me,* you will become weak and wimpy. If all you do is live in the *correct me,* you will become hard and mean. But if you combine them, you will grow up in the right structure of God.

Spend time in God's Word. It may be dry at first, but it's priming the pump of the Word. His Word is light, life, health and strength. If you don't put the Word into your spirit, you will not be able to reach your high calling and do what is right.

Psalm 119:11 says, "Thy word have I hid in mine heart that I might not sin against thee." If there is no Word in your heart, you are going to sin against God.

You see, when you are under stress and spiritual attack, what is in you is going to come out. If you have not put the Word in you, when pressure comes, whatever is in you will manifest.

If you put the Word in your spirit, it cleanses you, regenerates you, renews you, strengthens you and builds you so that when pressure hits, instead of goop coming out, the Word comes out. The principles of God come out. The strength of God comes out of your spirit.

- Develop a consistent prayer life.

How much time do you need to spend in prayer to make yourself strong? You have to figure that out for yourself, and it will be different for each one of us. But allow time in your life to commune with God. You have to go to the Source of life if you want to live a strong life.

Make sure you pray not only in English but in tongues as well. Why? Jude 20 says, "Beloved, [build] up yourselves on your most holy faith, praying in the Holy Ghost."

Paul told the Corinthians, "He that speaketh in an unknown tongue edifieth himself" (1 Cor. 14:4).

Most people probably haven't developed a strong personal prayer life. They depend on corporate prayer in the church. Don't do that. Don't ride the corporate prayer and expect it to be enough to strengthen your spirit. Let that be a little icing on the cake of your prayer life.

You say, "But, Roberts, I'm busy."

Well, so is the devil. He's busy seeking whom he may devour and busy looking for an entrance into your life. Praying in the Holy Ghost makes you strong.

Praying in your prayer language accomplishes many different things in your life. There is the intercessional side of tongues, where you are praying on behalf of another in the Spirit. There is also the combative role of tongues. Right now we are focusing on the role of tongues to build up your spirit. (In chapter nine we will take a look at the various operations of tongues in your life.)

If you don't tell your body what to do, it will keep you from building a strong spirit and living a productive life for the kingdom of God.

But wait a minute. We're getting ahead of ourselves. We'll get to the body — and how to keep it under control — in chapter five. For now, let's take an in-depth look at this wonderful yet almost inexplicable part of man called the spirit.

THREE

YOUR SPIRIT, GOD'S CANDLE

Our golden text for the school of the Spirit — or how to be led by the Spirit — is Romans 8:14: "For as many as are led by the Spirit of God, they are the sons of God."

Now the word many gives me the understanding that there are some who won't do this, who won't choose to be led by the Spirit. Remember, it's a choice.

Following the Leader

We must never lose the ability of being led, or following the Spirit's leading. We were created to be led by something. During all those years when you were led by sin, you did whatever you wanted. Suddenly, as a new Christian, you didn't want to do that — you had been born again and wanted to follow the Lord.

It's interesting how many people rebel against following or being led by the Spirit of God. I believe it is an early assault. The devil knows that if he can get you not to follow the Word and the leading of the Holy Spirit — who is sent by the Father to guide you into all truth — he can wreak havoc in your life and keep you from your great potential in Christ Jesus.

So the devil tries to play this game with you and get you to quit following. He tries to persuade you that following is bad and that you should be the master of your own life, when in fact it was what or *who* you were following that was wrong, not the following itself.

You never stop following — you just change guides. You change who you worship and who you follow. When we come into the Christian life, we must follow the Word, the Spirit and His leadings, just as we used to follow temptation. Only we didn't call it temptation; we just called it I-want-to.

A born-again person who is not led by the Spirit of God is sure to live in second-rate blessings, second-rate opportunities, second-rate activities. God never leads you into anything that is second-rate. He always leads you into the first, the best and the ultimate.

God never has a plan B — you're the one who usually has to have a plan B. When you live by faith and by the Spirit of God, you don't have to worry about plan B. God's best — His perfect plan A — will be fulfilled in your life.

This Little Light

Let's go to the book of Proverbs and look at a key passage of Scripture about the spirit of man:

> The spirit of man is the candle of the Lord, searching all the inward parts of the belly [or spirit] (Prov. 20:27).

If the spirit of man is "the candle of the Lord," that means the human spirit is where God sends His light. The light from this candle will illuminate the path you are to take — God's chosen path for your life. It lights your path so you can see the road signs telling you to go right or left, or the danger sign that is there to give you a warning.

But what exactly is the spirit of man? And how can God lead it? To answer that, let's take a look at the way man is created.

Look Who's Talking

One of the greatest struggles for most Christians is to understand who or what is talking to them. Which part of their makeup is speaking? How can they be sure the leading they sense is not their head or their flesh? How can they tell it is the Spirit of God?

Right off the bat, let me tell you that this discernment isn't automatic. We are responsible for developing our spirits to the point where we can hear God for ourselves. This is God's desire. This is miraculous. This is supernatural. This is greater than having a prophet give you a word.

If you want to be supernatural, learn to be led. I'm not against ministry from other people. But I'm also not dependent upon them. I can hear God for myself. I can follow God inside. You can develop that too.

> Rejoice evermore. Pray without ceasing. In everything give thanks: for this is the will of God in Christ Jesus concerning you. Quench not the Spirit. Despise not prophesyings. Prove all things; hold fast that which is good. Abstain from all appearance of evil. And the very God of peace sanctify you wholly; and I pray God your whole spirit and soul and body be preserved blameless unto the coming of our Lord Jesus Christ (1 Thess. 5:16-23).

Now from this verse it's very clear that there are three distinct parts to every human being. Scientists dissect frogs and everything else to find out what they are made of, but they can't figure out what man is made of because they can't find the spirit under their microscope.

But we can discover from our Creator how He made us, because God is not hiding anything. I believe He does not hold back information or truth that you need in your life.

One Being, Three Parts

God made us, and in His Word He told us how He made us. He said we are made up of three parts: spirit, soul and body.

One of these three parts will dominate your life. You are a spirit that owns a mind that lives in a body. That is the best way of describing how we are made. Another way to put it is, you are a spirit that owns a computer called the mind that lives in a body.

Let's look at some scriptures that show the distinction between these three parts, or how the apostles of the early church saw the difference.

In Philippians 1:21-24 Paul is speaking: "For to me to live is Christ, and to die is gain. But if I live in the flesh, this is the fruit of my labour: yet what I shall choose I wot not. For I am in a strait betwixt two, having a desire to depart, and to be with Christ; which is far better: nevertheless to abide in the flesh is more needful for you."

Now notice in these verses that Paul talked about staying in his flesh on the earth vs. going on to heaven. By the way he talked, it's clear he expected to still be living on the other side. His spirit was going to be living. His body would be dead, but he, the real Paul, was going to be alive. He knew what was going to happen — he saw the difference between the two.

In 2 Corinthians 4:16 he refers to two distinct parts: "For which cause we faint not; but though our outward man perish, yet the inward man is renewed day by day."

Peter recognized the distinction of the spirit as well: "But let it be the hidden man of the heart" (1 Pet. 3:4). The hidden man of the heart is the spirit.

The Inward Man

With your spirit you contact the spiritual realm — whether it is God's Spirit or the demonic realm. You do not contact the spiritual realm out of your physical senses or your soul.

Your spirit, or what Paul calls "the inward man," is the part of you that God speaks to. He doesn't talk to your soul or your mind. That's why people who aren't born again say, "How can you hear from God? What do you mean, you hear the voice of God? I've never heard the voice of God."

But how can they hear the voice of God when they are dead on the inside? That's why they want an audible voice, a burning bush, lightning in the sky. Because the only way they can perceive communicating to God, or hearing from God, is by their physical senses.

God doesn't talk to computers. It's foolish to think God is going to talk to something He made for you to use and not bother to talk to you. Can you imagine what it would be like if God came to your house and talked to your blender and thought it was you? Come and pull up a chair in front of your GE appliance and say, "Hi, how are you doing? I just wanted to come by and see how you are doing. I have a word for you today."

And you're standing there saying, "I'm over here."

That's what many people expect when they don't understand how God leads and speaks to us. They want God to talk to the blender and not to them. That's what your soul is — sort of like an appliance, something we use. I'm not trying to degrade it, I'm just trying to put it in its right place in your life. Thank God that He gave us a soul. We will get to that in a minute. But God does not speak to something that you own — He speaks to who you are, the real you. And people who are not trained to be led by the Spirit of God, and people who are not born again, have a hard time hearing from God because they are waiting for their soul to be hit with something. Or they expect their physical senses to feel something.

Your spirit is eternal. It is the one part of you that is born again.

What Does 'Born Again' Really Mean?

In John 3:1-7, Jesus is speaking to Nicodemus.

There was a man of the Pharisees, named Nicodemus, a ruler of the Jews: The same came to Jesus by night, and said unto him, Rabbi, we know that thou art a teacher come from God: for no man can do these miracles that thou doest except God be with him. Jesus answered and said unto him, Verily, verily, I say unto thee, Except a man be born again, he cannot see the kingdom of God.

Nicodemus saith unto him, How can a man be born when he is old? can he enter the second time into his mother's womb, and be born?

Jesus answered, Verily verily, I say unto thee, Except a man be born of water and of the Spirit, he cannot enter into the kingdom of God. That which is born of the flesh is

> flesh; and that which is born of the Spirit is spirit. Marvel not that I said unto thee, Ye must be born again.

When you are born again, you don't get a brand-new, baby-skin face. You keep the same old rough one you have right now. Your age doesn't go back to age one. It's your spirit that is reborn. Your body stays the same, and your soul has to be renewed, but your spirit is born again — not your head and not your body.

Paul wrote in 2 Corinthians 5:17, "Therefore if any man be in Christ, he is a new creature."

Being in Christ does not make you another type of human being in the sense of physical form. But you are a new creature, a new person on the inside. When someone is born again, their desires — their nature — should change as a sign of the new birth.

When a person is truly born again, their whole being is affected. There comes a change in their motivation, a change in their conduct, a change in their vocabulary. When you are born again, there should be a change, or I would doubt if you are born again.

Now it may be a small change in the beginning, or it may be big. I've seen some who began with a small change, but in time they kept growing, and the change got greater.

Let's look at the rest of verse 17: "Therefore if any man be in Christ, he is a new creature: old things are passed away; behold, all things are become new."

You renew your mind, and you keep your body under subjection. Your body has no conscience — it just has wants.

Let's review: With my spirit I contact the spiritual realm, and with it I can be in contact with God; with my body I contact the physical realm with my senses; and with my soul I contact the intellectual realm.

They say that to be forewarned is to be forearmed, so let me warn you now before we look into the realm of the soul — it can be one of your most dangerous enemies if you allow it to stay unrenewed.

FOUR

CONTROLLING THE SOUL

In the last chapter we discussed the different parts of the human makeup: the spirit, soul and body of man. We dealt with the spirit, which is the real you. God does not talk to your soul — He talks to you. That's why the Bible says, "As many as are led by the Spirit of God, they are the sons of God." It's done by His inward working in you.

Most folks live out of their mind and think it is their spirit. That's why they are always in trouble. You can't figure out spiritual difficulties with reasoning. It is done by spiritual reception and God's leading you in your inward man, giving you instructions about what to do.

The moment you are filled with the Holy Spirit, demons abruptly come against you and try to gain entry into your life to render you ineffective for God's kingdom. But the Spirit of God woos and nudges you and speaks to you gently. He never violates the will He gave you.

God is not a violater of the human will. He is a respecter of the human will. But demons love to violate both God's will and the human will — which is a component of the part of man called the soul.

Dissecting the Soul

What makes up the human soul? Mainly there are three parts, but I will give you five: 1) the will, 2) the emotions, 3) the intellect, 4) the imagination and 5) the memory.

The will. Have you ever desired to do something, but you chose not to do it? That was your will in action. When an evil spirit comes at your soul, his goal is to take hold of your will.

He may use all the other aspects of the soul to get to the will, but his goal is the will of a human. He may enter in through the emotions. He may enter in through the intellect, the vain imaginations or the memory and then capture the will. But his goal in the battle of the soul is always the will.

Usually a demon cannot just come and capture the will right up front. He's crafty, and he knows that if he uses the other avenues, he can most likely gain access to the will.

A demon knows that if he gets the will of a human, he'll be able to achieve his ultimate goal: to get back at God. He knows he will have the ability to corrupt that person by injecting his own evil, twisted nature into their thought patterns.

Once an evil spirit has the will of a human, that person no longer has any resistant power. Your will is your resister and your receiver. Your will is the door you choose to open or close. It's your choice. That is what God gave Adam and Eve in the beginning.

God told them, "Don't eat of this certain tree." But they chose to do it.

You may say, "Why did God let them do it?"

God told them what to do, but He gave them the freedom to obey or disobey. Why would God do that?

God doesn't like robots — He likes real beings. He gave mankind a free will. That makes us real. That means we choose to say, "God, I love you; I will obey You," and it's not a program out of a computer system.

When God gave us the gift of free will, it caused us to be real.

The emotions. The human emotions, or feelings, are the main entry gate by which demons access the human soul. This is also the number-one part of the human soul that people mistake for their spirit, because the spirit man does feel. The spirit man does have senses — if you want to use that word — relating to the spiritual realm. But the emotions of the soul are different.

The majority of Christians confuse this one compartment of the soul with the Spirit's direction. They are led according to their feelings but call it being led by the Spirit.

This is especially risky because many times in following God, you will feel one thing and actually be led in the opposite direction. It would be good if you could get the two together, but sometimes you can feel one thing that is totally opposite of the way God is leading you.

The emotional realm is also where the greatest scars of the soul are found. This is where the majority of human sorrow still speaks and moves and clamors for attention. Some people store up so many sorrows they become emotionally handicapped — the traumas were too much for them.

Jesus is still the healer of the soul. "He restoreth my soul" (Ps. 23:3). In other words, He brings it back to the way it should be.

The intellect. This third main compartment of the soul encompasses your intellect, your reasoning and your logic. Most humans fall into the trap of confusing their emotions with their spirit, but some people are more intellect-driven. They reason and analyze and discuss and think, think, think.

Your brain will subordinate anything that is superior to it if you allow it. It will take God and put Him under you. A rebellious, unrenewed soul will do that.

That's why you have people who, in the name of God, even turn the gospel into an intellectual thing. They always have another question. An absolute they can't take unless it's a *Thomas* kind of absolute — see, hear, touch, know scientifically.

Many times Christian universities become dominated by intellectualism. The enemy may use questionings, logic and reason to disqualify the absolutes of the Bible. The faculty will sit there and discuss why this and that is not relevant for today.

How could a Christian university — or an individual Christian — get to that point? By not keeping the intellect submitted to the Word of God. You have to bring in the Word of God as the check and balance, the standard. Because the soul is always in a fight. Galatians 6 talks about this. A constant war rages between your flesh and your spirit, your soul and your spirit.

The soul wants to be king in your life. It doesn't want to be quiet and submissive when you are hearing from God and praying to God. It wants you to go into the intellectual mode and think through everything.

There is no such thing as an intellectual conversion. Jesus didn't say, "Think about it." He told us to receive the new birth by faith.

John Wesley, back in the 1700s, talked about people who mentally assent to something. They think it through, and they mentally agree, but it has not been made real in their heart. It has not brought about a change in their being.

But the Bible never talks about the soul in the new birth — it talks only about the heart, or the spirit of man.

There is nothing wrong with education, but you don't have to be educated to be a great person in God. Education is good as long as you keep it submitted to the standard of the Word.

Sometimes people think they have to be highly educated to be obedient. What about the rooster that crowed and convicted Peter? It's amazing how many animals God uses throughout the Bible to do things.

If God can use a rooster, there is hope for you. Never think that you are not qualified — you are qualified. You're better qualified than that rooster, or Balaam's donkey.

Keep your intellect submitted to the Word. Paul warned Timothy not to "give heed to fables and endless genealogies" (1 Tim. 1:4). God has absolutes. When in doubt, go to His Word and settle the issue there.

Imaginations. Everybody has imaginations. There are good imaginations, and there are also what the Bible calls "vain imaginations." This is also a part of your soul — imagining. Paul, writing to the Corinthians, told us what to do with vain imaginations.

> For the weapons of our warfare are not carnal, but mighty through God to the pulling down of strong holds; casting down imaginations, and every high thing that exalteth itself against the knowledge of God, and bringing into captivity every thought to the obedience of Christ (2 Cor. 10:4-5).

Oftentimes ambition builds its castles. Fantasy also lives in the realm of imagination. There is not a true reality there. Imagination is good — it was given to us by God — but it too must stay in submission to the Word and our spirit.

Sometimes people claim to have a vision, but it's really an imagination. This is because they have a religious soul — not a renewed mind and a restored soul. Most of the time a false vision has its source in a vain imagination. It's the soul seeking to become dominant over the spirit by fooling you into agreeing with the vain imagination it has conjured up.

You have to keep your imaginations in right order.

The memory. I think the memory is the second main door by which the devil captures people because most of the time we remember the bad. Even though the good is present, it is not always dominant unless you renew your mind.

Renewing your mind means making your memory remember the good things of your life and not just the bad. You could always think of all the people who did you wrong, but why not remember the ones who blessed you? If you don't watch it, a negative memory can dominate the conduct of your life.

Keep your memory in check in accordance to Philippians 4:8.

> Finally, brethren, whatsoever things are true, whatsoever things are honest, whatsoever things are just, whatsoever things are pure, whatsoever things are lovely, whatsoever things are of good report; if there be any virtue, and if there be any praise, think on these things.

The word *think* talks of the soul — the human mind. So you can say that every part of your soul should be in the realm of these things listed here. Let's go back and look at them again.

Tell your intellect to quit living in theory all the time, and to come over to fact and truth. Think on things that are honest, pure, lovely; think on things that are of a good report, that are virtuous or of value. Things that have praise — think on these things.

Many people are held captive by a bad past, and

their controlling memory stops them from living in the present, let alone reaching into the future. We all have bad experiences in our past. They were real, they are there — and we can justify in our thinking why we should not let them go.

It's up to you to take charge of your soul. You are going to have to say, "Now, memory, you remember what is good." It's so easy to think of all the bad things that have happened, but you also need to remember the good things God has done in your life.

The Divine Splicer

For the word of God is quick, and powerful, and sharper than any twoedged sword, piercing even to the dividing asunder of soul and spirit, and of the joints and marrow, and is a discerner of the thoughts and intents of the heart (Heb. 4:12).

Staying in the Word helps you divide in your life what is of your soul and what is of your spirit — or what is right and what is wrong. Putting the Word of God in you gives you the ability to rightly divide circumstances, decisions, motives, intents of the heart — all these things.

Many times people have the soul and the spirit mixed up. That's why they can't tell the difference between God's voice and the voice of their human spirit. That's why they don't know the voice of God from the voice of their own head talking. They can't hear Him because they let His voice get mixed in with their own thoughts. It's a mix that should not be allowed.

The spirit and the soul should cooperate — but not be mixed.

Saving the Soul

The new birth brings about an immediate change in your being. Your inward man is changed instantaneously. But your soul does not have the same quick change.

I'll never forget once when Billy Joe Daugherty, pastor of Victory Christian Center in Tulsa, Oklahoma, asked a man who had gotten saved one week earlier to come up and say something to the whole congregation. You could tell the man was still newly saved. He got up, grinning from ear to ear, and said, "This is the damndest life I've ever had. It's the greatest thing — everybody should have it!"

Now we all knew what he meant. But there was a major problem in the middle of his word of testimony. You could tell from his inward man that there had come a change — and he loved it. But his soul needed some help.

When people get born again, immediately their inner man will change, and they will love how they feel on the inside. But then there are these other two parts that they have to deal with — the soul and the body.

The soul has to be saved. Now, how is the soul saved? Romans 12 holds the answer. It is by the renewing of the mind through the Word. I wish I could tell you that when we are born again our soul gets revamped right along with our spirit. But it doesn't. Whether you like it or not, this is the way it's going to have to be.

You are going to have to do your own renewing of your mind.

> Be not conformed to this world: but be ye transformed by the renewing of your mind, that ye may prove what is that good, and acceptable, and perfect, will of God (Rom. 12:2).

God made it very clear in this particular verse that transformation of your soul comes about through the renewing of your mind. If you are lazy — or rebellious — and don't renew your mind, you will still be a Christian, but at best you'll live your life half in the Spirit and half in the flesh, or your carnal nature.

You can't operate half Spirit and half flesh.

That's where a lot of people are today. They operate half Spirit and half flesh, so they get nowhere — except right where they are. They get just enough Spirit to maintain a moderate level of victory but enough carnality to keep them from going on. They never get enough Spirit to make progress.

A Word About Carnal Christians

Have you ever heard the term *carnal Christian?* You can define it like this: A carnal Christian is one who is born again but who never renewed his mind or disciplined his physical body to come in line with the new birth rights and privileges.

Carnal Christians stay over in the realm of the soul and the physical. They have a born-again experience, but they are not living it. They are not living out of the fruit of the Spirit — out of the character of God. Their mind is still unrenewed. They think the same way, talk the same way, act the same way. They couldn't tell the difference between the Holy Spirit's voice and a demon's voice if their lives depended on it.

Carnal Christians know they are born again because they have asked Jesus into their heart; they believe they received salvation, and thus they have. But after that they quit.

But to be a totally transformed person you have to deal with all three parts — your spirit, soul and body.

He Restoreth My Soul

Believe it or not, the Old Testament has something to say about transforming your soul. Hold your place in Romans and go to Psalm 23. Here's a world-famous psalm, and tucked away in verse 3 — most people just read right over it — is this nugget: "He restoreth my soul."

If your soul didn't need restoring, God wouldn't be in the business of doing it. We have all types of people in the church. Their number-one problem is their head. Yes, they are born again, but they don't spend time correcting their thought patterns. They don't spend time renewing their mind.

Renewing your mind is very basic: You renew it by putting the Word of God into your soul and meditating upon the Word. If you do that often enough, you will begin to notice a change in the way you think. Your thoughts will be filtered through the Word of God.

So far we have examined the first two parts of our makeup: the spirit and the soul. We have established that with the spirit we contact the spiritual realm, or are led by the Spirit. With our soul we contact the intellectual realm.

Now let's take a look at the third part of your makeup — the body — with which you contact the physical realm and the senses.

FIVE

BATTLING THE BODY

W hen you were a baby, no one had to tell you when you were hungry, did they? You knew because your stomach growled. Nor did you need to be told when your diaper was dirty, or when you were too warm or too cold. You experienced those sensations through your physical body — whether you wanted to or not.

As spirit beings living inside bodies, we contact the physical realm — the realm of the natural — through our bodies. But, unfortunately, when we are born again, our bodies don't get overhauled the way our spirits do.

The human body is fearfully and wonderfully made (Ps. 139:14). It is a remarkable "house" for your spirit to dwell in while you're on this earth. I like to call it a "body suit." If we go to the moon, we must wear a space suit. Otherwise, because of a lack of gravity, our bodies would leave the moon. The space suit holds our bodies to the surface of the moon.

The human body — your body suit — works the same way. It houses your spirit while you're here on earth. It holds your spirit man to the earth. But if your body dies, the spirit leaves. It cannot stay, because it is no longer tethered to the earth.

Your Body as a Holy Vessel

Your human body is the vessel by which the Spirit speaks and moves. The human vessel has always been important to God. Stephen in the book of Acts understood this principle. He yielded his body to the Spirit of the Lord and allowed his voice to be used to convict those around him. The religious leaders of the day had resisted the Holy Spirit up to that point. But Acts 6:10 states that they could not resist His influence when He spoke through the human vessel Stephen.

Stephen ultimately surrendered his earthly vessel for the cause of Christ.

Jesus wants to live through your human body. He wants to demonstrate His compassion for individuals through you. He desires for the Scriptures to come alive through your mortal flesh. And your body is the vessel by which the gospel is carried into the nations.

So the body serves a tremendous function in God's kingdom: It houses your spirit, it is a vessel through which the Holy Spirit ministers, and it carries the Word of God to an unbelieving world. But it can be your lifelong enemy if you don't discipline it.

Your body has only wants and desires — no thinking abilities or emotions. It is a seeker of its own pleasures. The only time it stops is when you stop it or it breaks down from old age or ill use. Some people let their bodies smoke cigarettes. Some let other people use their bodies for immoral purposes. Some people turn their livers into swiss cheese by pouring alcohol into their bodies over a long period of time. No wonder our bodies break down.

But God in His Word has something to say about your body and its proper function for His kingdom.

A Living Sacrifice

Romans 12:1: "I beseech you therefore, brethren, by the mercies of God, that ye present your bodies a living sacrifice, holy, acceptable unto God, which is your reasonable service."

Paul says, "I beseech you therefore, *brethren,* by the mercies of God, that ye present your bodies." He is talking to Christians. Who does the presenting? You. Not we — you. Not your wife, not your husband; it's you.

"Present your bodies a living sacrifice," Paul says.

To the person who is born again, who has lived their life with God, dying the physical death is a graduation. It's a continuation — a going on. That's the way we need to look at it. Our soul does grieve, but our spirit can rejoice.

That's why people who are not born again think Christians are nuts. They say, "How can you say 'Praise God!' when a person dies?" Well, it's because they've finished their course. They've run the race, and they went on to be with the Lord. It's only sad to the soul because of the loneliness of the people left behind.

The last few words of Romans 12:1 make it clear whose responsibility it is to keep the body in line: It is "your reasonable service."

Your body is your responsibility. What your body does or does not do is your responsibility— nobody else's. You can blame it on everybody else in the country. You can blame it on your past, your present, your future. But it still comes down to this: Your body is your responsibility.

It does not think— it just craves. It mainly wants three things: sex, food and comfort. These are the three things your physical man wants in large doses. Every time I teach on this, everybody starts to laugh. I know it sounds funny. But it's true.

Did you notice that all three of these cravings originate in the senses? No wonder the world is blitzed by TV ads, billboards, magazines, videos and other material to stimulate the senses of your human body. The devil knows how to get your mind off the things of God by going after your flesh. You see a great big juicy Whopper on a TV commercial, and suddenly you want one. You crave a Whopper. The same is true for comfort and luxury. The desire for higher levels of comfort and ease is fed by advertisements that appeal to your senses in this area.

I don't have to tell you how much our society panders to the sensual. Sex sells, and it is dangled before our eyes everywhere we turn. This is probably the number one area of temptation for believers today.

The sexual drive in you was placed there by God. And it is kept in line by boundaries outlined in the Bible, according to moral codes. But the regulating of your physical activity is done by your spirit and your mind. If you leave your body to itself, it'll do what it wants, when it wants, with whomever it wants and not feel guilty.

Your soul will feel guilty, and your spirit will feel grieved. But your body won't feel guilty. Your body does not see the wedding band, which signifies that someone is in covenant with another. If you've given your physical body freedom to do what it wants, it's only when you wake up and your soul comes back into check that you have regrets.

We must be careful what we gaze upon and what we listen to. When the flesh yields to sensual distractions, it cannot please God. Guard your senses, as they are the entrance to your human body.

Keeping the Body Under Subjection

Paul wrote in 1 Corinthians 9:27:

> I keep under my body, and bring it into subjection: lest that by any means, when I have preached to others, I myself should be a castaway.

Who does what? Paul says, "I keep." It isn't we,

them or the church. I keep my body. It is my responsibility to keep it in moral order, physical health and so forth.

An evil spirit seeks to find dwelling in the physical. His goal is to dwell in the spirit of man — to take possession of it, or of the soul. He'll take any part of you he can get. That's why a Christian who is born again cannot have demons in their spirit, but they can have them in their mind and body. Because your mind has to be renewed. If you don't keep renewing your mind, then the devil can take advantage of it.

Likewise, if you don't keep your body under subjection, he can take advantage of the looseness of your physical appetites and oblige them, and by obliging those appetites he can find entrance, or a degree of control over you.

When you are being led by the Spirit, all three parts of your makeup have a voice. Your spirit has a voice, your soul has a voice and your body has a voice.

The voice of your soul is reasoning, the voice of your spirit is faith and the voice of your body is the physical senses. You have to know which one is speaking, because some people get them all mixed up. No wonder they end up in trouble. They try to make the decision of getting married based on the physical. All your body wants is sex. It doesn't want to live a life of commitment and build a home and a family. It just craves physical gratification.

Let's stop and look again at our golden text for the school of the Spirit:

As many as are led by the Spirit of God, they are the sons of God (Rom. 8:14).

You desire to be led by the Spirit of God or you wouldn't be reading this book. Well, you have taken the first step toward getting there. God recognizes your desire, and He will honor it.

We've covered the three distinct parts of man — the spirit, soul and body — and how each one can help or hinder you in the school of the Spirit. But now let's move on beyond the milk and get into the meat of the Word. It only gets better.

SIX

THE NECESSITY FOR SPIRITUAL HUNGER

Y ou can learn to be led by the Holy Spirit whether you have been a Christian for two months or twenty years. The first requirement is spiritual hunger. You may be able to fake spirituality at church, but you can't fool God. He knows if you're hungry or not. And that hunger makes all the difference.

Jesus said in the Sermon on the Mount, "Blessed are they which do hunger and thirst after righteousness: for they shall be filled" (Matt. 5:6).

And in Luke 6:20-21, "[Jesus] lifted up his eyes on his disciples, and said, Blessed be ye poor: for yours is the kingdom of God. Blessed are ye that hunger now: for ye shall be filled. Blessed are ye that weep now: for ye shall laugh."

You Have to Be Hungry

The first step to flowing with the Holy Spirit on a daily basis is this spiritual hunger and thirst that Jesus described. When I first started walking with God, there was such a hunger on the inside of me. That hunger is still there, and it is growing. I hunger for more of God. Back in my childhood where it began, I knew I wanted God big — not small. I wanted Him big.

There has to be a yearning for more of God deep down in your spirit man, regardless of whether He ever does a miracle or not. Grandma developed that in me. She made me eat righteousness until my appetite desired more of it. She made me eat the Word. She made me read my Bible from cover to cover every year as long as I was under her authority.

Grandma trained me. Now that I am older I have not departed from the way, because she developed this in me first — a hunger and thirst after righteousness.

How to Develop the Hunger

What did Grandma do to develop spiritual hunger in me? I believe this is the first step, and I'm going to drill it in you because if you don't get this one, you can't climb higher: She made me devour the Scriptures. If I didn't read them, I was hearing them. She played gospel tapes in every room. She had the Word of God invading our home. My sister and I heard nothing but that which was righteous. She didn't allow us to associate with people who did not want the things of God.

A lot of people try to do in their home what my grandmother did in ours, and they have problems because they don't have love. You can't do it successfully without a love for God and a love for your family. That's the oil in the engine. If you don't have love you will have problems.

That's why I often receive letters from teens saying: "My mother is making me read the Bible. I am getting sick of it, and I want to backslide, even though I know it's not right. Why do I feel this way?"

It's not their fault, it's Mom and Dad's fault.

I don't write them a letter back; I write to the parents of that child and say: "Listen to me: You're not doing it right, so quit it. You have to have love."

My upbringing worked because my mother and grandmother loved us. The first thing I heard in the morning was Grandma preaching. And after I got home at night, Grandma was preaching and turning tapes over. I kept hearing the truth. The natural man has a built-in desire for truth. It wants reality. She gave it to us over and over and over.

The day came when God told her she could be released from drilling the Bible into us. She said, "Now it's up to you to receive your own revelations, to receive your own knowledge, and for you to keep that desire which I have developed in you."

By that time we had reached the point where we

liked it. We liked hearing the Bible stories. We liked hearing about the deep things of God.

Passionate Hunger

On my first trip to Africa, we took candy for the children. Some of them had never seen a piece of peppermint. They didn't know what chocolate was. They had heard about chocolate and butterscotch, and they had developed a hunger for it. But they had never tasted it.

The guide who brought us into the little village said, "Now, you be careful of that candy because they will jump you for it."

I pulled the bag of candy out of my pocket and asked, "You want these?" I had three pieces of candy in my hand, but they knew I had more. They had been desiring candy for years, and here was an American missionary holding his hand out, saying, "Do you want a piece of candy?"

They could not understand a word I said, but they knew what I meant. They knew what I had in my pocket, though some could not see what was in my hand. Twenty-five children, and me with one hand holding up three pieces of candy.

Someone said, "Roberts, be careful."

I thought, What can these little kids do to me?

I brought my hand down, watching the candy to see how fast it would go. I didn't know my fingers would go with it. They hit so fast, and they were hanging on to my fingers and pulling them in every direction.

They hungered after that candy. They wanted it. And when they saw it, they reached out and grabbed it — it was theirs. Three children got it. It made the others mad. But I was scared to put out my hand anymore. I wanted a hand when I came back to America. I didn't want to be torn apart by African children while I was trying to give them candy.

I got in the truck and closed the door. I said to the person on the passenger side, "Here's the bag of candy. When I count to three, you grab as much as you can and throw it out the window. That way we'll be safe."

So we threw it, and those kids went after it. They were all over the car screaming "Candy!" in their native language.

The point of my story is this: If you do not hunger after the things of God like those children hungered after that candy, when the things of God do come, you won't recognize them.

Something is happening in the realm of the Spirit, and my spirit knows about it — it's hungering for it. So when it gets here, I'll know what it is, and I'll jump for it and get into it.

But so many people do not have any hunger at all, and when the things of God come, they say, "Oh, it's just *those* people. They're getting too involved with it; they're just overly dramatic."

Yet those were the things of God. And the naysayers missed it.

Why did so many people miss the charismatic movement? Why are they still missing the moves of God that are happening in our midst right now? Because they did not hunger and thirst for the things of God long before they ever came.

The African children were hungering after that candy, waiting for the next white person to come through with a bag of butterscotch. That's the way we need to be with the things of God. We're waiting for the next wave. We've enjoyed what we've had, but we are still hungry for more. We want more of God. We want more of His presence.

You come to Him with desire, you sit down, and you think on it. That's the way you develop the spiritual hunger you need. The devil won't stop you. God will not start you. It's all up to you.

You don't have grandmas and parents to force-feed you anymore. You just have you. And you have to do this if you want to flow with the Holy Spirit.

I remember walking the floor and saying, "God, I want more of you. Holy Spirit, flow through me. Holy Spirit, lead me, teach me, guide me. I want more of You. I want all I can get, and then I want some more."

You ask, "How long did you have to walk the floor and pray until you really had the desire?"

For months. Every day I would walk the floor and say it. And if it didn't come out of my mouth, I was meditating about it. I made myself do this.

Be Spiritually Fit

It's a spiritual exercise to develop your inward man. If you exercise your physical body, you know from experience that it doesn't get firm and muscular by itself. You don't even expect it to. You just accept the fact that if you want a strong body you have to do certain things. You have to give it a good workout on a regular basis.

Your body doesn't always like it when you push it past the comfort zone. And it will protest and kick and scream and be sore for days, but pretty soon it will start to like it because being physically fit feels good.

Jesus said those who "hunger and thirst after right-eousness" will be filled (Matt. 5:6).

If you're not hungry, walk the floor like I did and confess. Believers need hunger. They should be starving all the time. Once you get full of this glory, you should already be reaching for the next glory.

Until you get this one thing, the other things won't come. They go together. Hunger is the bottom line. That's where everything starts. You have to hunger. And when the things of God start to come, reach out and grab them with your faith.

Hunger causes you to go to the furthest point to get satisfied. It will cause you to go out there with every-thing you have, not considering anything else. That's the way you have to be with the things of God.

How long do you have to hunger like that before God will answer you? Until it's a proven hunger.

If you're to go far in the realm of the Spirit, you need to start now. Develop a hunger and thirst in your spirit. Not tomorrow — today.

From Glory to Glory

Those who "hunger and thirst after righteousness" will be filled.

To go on to the next glory you have to be filled first. God does the filling. He satisfies your longing. But He always leaves room for you to hunger after something more.

A lot of people get filled and then stay in that one glory. They keep eating that same food. They do not open their eyes to see what is next. They do not walk in faith for the next thing that God desires for them.

But that's the way God created spiritual hunger to be. While you're eating and feasting on what He's given you, your eyes are still looking for and desiring the next glory of God.

God said that's what we need to do before we ever flow in the Spirit of God. Hunger causes us to flow beautifully. Hunger causes you not to have any questions; you just devour it and go on.

People who are hungry don't ask where the food came from. They don't ask, "Who prepared this nice steak for me? Are you sure they prepared it the right way?" They just start eating it.

Spiritual hunger knows spiritual food. If you are hungry for a steak, you won't eat an empty milk carton. You know it's not food. Nobody has to tell you. It's the same with spiritual hunger.

It's not that complicated — developing the hunger, following the leading of the Spirit, flowing with God. We have to develop that before we can ever move on, before we go to the next glory. And when it hits, don't stop on that one glory. You'll lose ground.

I think of glory as a mountain leading up to heaven. You have the ability to climb it, and you are never to stop. Once you stop climbing, you start sliding backwards. There is no neutral ground. You will fall right back down and have to do it again.

Folks who think they've arrived eventually end up with nothing.

Be Spiritually Aggressive

Military leaders know that if you can starve a people you can rule a people. Marxist governments know that. They know that if they can seize a nation and starve its people, then when they do bring them food, the people will do anything they want and think exactly the way they want them to think.

That's why God has placed this in us. Because if we are desiring the things of God; if we are hungering after them, then we will be militant in getting them. We will break down the doors of darkness to get to the true light.

Hungry people are aggressive people. Spiritually hungry people are spiritually aggressive people. If you want the power of God in your life; if you want those things that you've heard talked about for years, then do what I've instructed you here. You'll never regret it.

I hungered, and I received. And I'm hungering for more. The deep calls to the deep (Ps. 42:7). If there is a deep calling, there has to be a depth to answer the call. If there is a hunger, there has to be something to satisfy that hunger.

If you are hungering for more of the Holy Spirit, there has to be more of Him to satisfy you. If you are hungering for more power, there has to be more power to receive. If you are hungering for more love, there has to be more love.

Hunger after the things of God. Don't hunger for anything else. Don't seek after anybody or anything but God. The Bible says that if you hunger after God, He will give all those things to you. God will see that you have everything you need in the natural. He says, "Seek ye first the kingdom of God, and his righteousness; and all these things shall be aded unto you" (Matt. 6:33).

There's more out there if you just open your hand. But how do you really walk in the Spirit? How do you move beyond the realm of the ordinary into the supernatural? By operating in God's "higher laws" — the laws of the Spirit.

SEVEN

OPERATING IN THE SPIRIT REALM

C hristianity is not a natural organization. It's not a formula. Christianity was born of the Spirit, and it operates on spiritual principles — principles that transcend the laws of the natural universe.

The men who promoted the gospel of Jesus Christ were men of the Spirit. Paul was so in tune with the Spirit that when they locked him up, an angel came and set him free. Whenever he walked into a city, devils would scream and come out. What scares devils? A person who walks with an understanding of his rights and privileges in Christ.

A Christian who knows how to stand on his privileges in Christ and come out the victor — that's what scares the devil. A person who is born again but lives in the flesh does not scare the devil. But a person who is born again and walks in the Spirit will tear up the devil every time.

Why? Because the person who lives in the Spirit knows spiritual principles, uses spiritual weapons and fights Satan on his territory. That's the big difference. The church of almighty God is on the offensive!

Paul said, "We wrestle not against flesh and blood, but against principalities, against powers" (Eph. 6:12). He annihilated all warfare of the flesh. He said, "If you wrestle with flesh and blood, sorry — you missed the whole boat. The enemy is still there."

It's time you began to operate in the Spirit every day of your life. You can't be in both kingdoms. You can't live in carnality and in the Spirit at the same time. It doesn't work. Both efforts will fail.

The greatest example throughout history of a man who operated in the realm of the Spirit is our Savior, Jesus. He is our great example that we are to follow. The things He said and did when He walked the earth, He is saying again to His church today, and we must begin to move in them.

The church is coming full circle. At the fall, mankind plunged downward from the level God created us to occupy. The moves and revivals throughout history began to carry us upward, and I believe we are now standing on the threshold of a new wave, as well as a dispensational change. I sense in my spirit that as the church travels further in the Spirit, the confrontations we meet will be increasingly like the one Jesus met when He was on the Sea of Galilee.

Take Authority in the Spirit

The Bible says in Mark 4:35-41:

> And the same day, when the even was come, he saith unto them, Let us pass over unto the other side. And when they had sent away the multitude, they took him even as he was in the ship. And there were also with him other little ships.
>
> And there arose a great storm of wind, and the waves beat into the ship, so that it was now full. And he was in the hinder part of the ship, asleep on a pillow: and they awake him, and say unto him, Master, carest thou not that we perish?
>
> And he arose, and rebuked the wind, and said unto the sea, Peace, be still. And the wind ceased, and there was a great calm. And he said unto them, Why are ye so fearful? How is it that ye have no faith? And they feared exceedingly, and said one to another, What manner of man is this, that even the wind and the sea obey him?

Here we have a boat with thirteen men in it — one of whom is fast asleep while the wind is blowing and the waves are crashing. But the other twelve men are scared stiff. They don't know what is going to happen, but their minds tell them they are about to die. They know their leader can perform miracles, so they wake Him up.

Now it's one thing for a man to sleep through a minor storm. But it is another thing for a man to sleep through a major storm. This was a major storm. So much so that it says, "The waves beat into the ship."

The boat was going to sink — they were going to die! They woke this Man up. He turned around to them and said, "How is it that ye have no faith!"

What a statement to make to people who are grasping for life! It's like saying, "What's wrong with you?" That's really what it meant. "What's wrong with you? I've been with you many days. I've taught you how to cast out devils, heal the sick, raise the dead and feed five thousand with one little lunch. Now you are scared of the wind and the waves — what's wrong with you? Why did you wake me up?"

But notice that in the same breath He calmed the storm. He turned around in the midst of that storm and said, "Peace, be still." And it happened.

We must learn, like our Savior, how to live in the world of the Spirit where we can take authority over situations, because we are heading for great confrontations in the earth and in the heavenlies. But the Bible teaches us everything we need to know about life in the Spirit.

Don't Touch It in the Natural

In our story we see twelve men who reacted to the storm in the flesh. You get in a boat, the winds come up, and waves are crashing into the boat. Meanwhile, you have a Man sleeping in the stern of the boat.

What would the mind tell you to do? It would say, "Get the buckets! Somebody do this; somebody do that!"

The mind will say, "What are the simple words 'Peace, be still' going to do in a raging storm?" It's the same way when you're praying in tongues and warring in the Spirit. Your mind doesn't understand, so it will say, "What are you doing? Don't you know this doesn't work? Don't you realize you look strange?"

But, you see, here's the track record of the mind: It will get you to lean into it, but when you finally let it have its way, it never works.

Devils are not your greatest threat. The greatest battle you will ever face is getting your head in line so you can face the devils. When you are caught between a rock and a hard place like those disciples, and everything around you looks bad — real bad — don't touch it in the natural. Touch it in the Spirit like Jesus did. Have faith in Spirit-actions.

Operating in the Spirit Realm

Notice Jesus didn't say it twice — "Peace, be still. Peace, be still." He said it once because that was all that was necessary. When you operate in the world of the Spirit, you can control natural circumstances for the glory of God. I didn't say for self gain. Carnality will try to slip in and get you to operate in the Spirit for your own glory.

Walking in the Spirit is the only way you are going to be able to stand in the storm of this world and say with confidence, "Peace, be still," to your home, to your business, to your ministry, and still come out on top. As I said in the introduction, this message is more than just a sweet little teaching. It is your future safety, as the ark was to Noah and his family.

Know this with every fiber of your being: Anyone who does not walk in the Spirit shall suffer. Because when you walk in the Spirit, you know things supernaturally. You know how to confront devils and win before they ever cause havoc in the natural.

We are not dealing with headache devils anymore — we are dealing with princes of power. The forces the church is coming up against today are powerful.

We have to learn to operate on a spiritual level all the time — not half Spirit-man and half carnal-man.

Spirit life is a command; it's not a suggestion. The Bible doesn't say, "If you decide to walk in the Spirit, you won't fulfill the lusts of the flesh." It says, "Walk in the Spirit, and ye shall not fulfill the lust of the flesh" (Gal. 5:16).

The Bible says you have been "translated" from darkness to light. It doesn't say you went and visited. It says you have changed residencies.

Over here in the realm of the Spirit, you have to live on the unseen resources of God. Your flesh fights you. "Go back over there where you know this works," it says, "where you can see it and feel it — where your mind is in charge."

That is where most Christians are today. They are in the head — in the mind. They don't want to rely on unseen resources that cause victory and success in every situation.

But when the devil is standing right in front of you, when the situation looks like a disaster, how are you going to deal with it — in the natural or in the Spirit?

That's the decision. Because when it looks horrible, most people want to go to the flesh. You have to incline yourself to the Spirit. You have to say, "All right, the Bible says it, and I'm going to believe it."

Never once in this storm did Jesus touch it with His mind. He never said, "John and Peter, start doing this or that." Most people would say, "Get your lifejacket on, and get to the raft!" But no. He attacked it in the Spirit. He spoke from His Spirit into the world of the Spirit, which caused those natural laws and events to align with the perfect will of God.

Your future depends upon your knowledge and your ability to operate in the Spirit realm on behalf of your life, your family, your business and your church for the glory of God.

Jesus activated the law of faith to calm the sea. People who do not operate in the Spirit are not really walking in the Spirit. Conversely, if you are in the Spirit, you are living by spiritual laws.

In the realm of the Spirit, everything hinges on faith in God. And that's the subject of our next lesson.

EIGHT

FAITH VS. RELIGION

Faith is a potent force. It's not a minor power; it's a major power in the life of a Christian. Everything we do in Christianity is done on the basis of faith in God.

You come into the kingdom by faith. You obtain the blessings by faith. You overcome the evil one by faith. You never get to the point where you have too much faith. You can always use more.

The Bible says "the just shall live by faith" (Heb. 10:38). Faith and logic never get along. Logic said,

Peter, don't step out on the water. You'll sink.
  Faith said, Do it!
  Logic said, Lazarus is decaying in that cave.
  Faith said, Call him out!
  And he came out.
  Faith is expectancy. It is released by our words and actions. The prayer of faith is released with expectancy that God will do what His Word promises us. Religion is the enemy of faith. So it follows that religious prayers achieve the opposite of faith prayers: nothing.

Religious Prayer

The number-one type of religious prayer is what people call "the attitude of prayer." With the attitude of prayer, you don't really pray, you just look like you do. It's a form of godliness with no true power behind it.

Now you can rationalize this all you want, but I don't like rationalizing when it comes to spirituality. The Bible says it, and we do it. The Bible says if we do this thing, it will happen. So be it. That's the way it is.

What is religion? The Bible defines it as "having a form of godliness, but denying the power thereof" (2 Tim. 3:5). It looks good, but there's no juice, no oil, no *pow!* to it. That's religion, and I hate it. Hatred is all right when it's toward the right thing. You don't hate people; you hate devils. You hate sin. When you hate the devil, your spirit develops such a love for God.

The second kind of religious prayer is when you say all the right things but have no true faith that God heard you and will answer you. You pray a prayer because you're a Christian, and you know it's the right thing to do.

People go through the motions of prayer all the time, and there's no faith. There's no power behind it. Faith is what makes prayers powerful. And whatever is not of faith is sin (Rom. 14:23).

Religion chokes faith if you let it. Religion hates faith. It says, Live by logic; live by reason; live by what you can accomplish in your own ability. Trust in the seen, not the unseen.

Faith should never diminish. It should always be abounding. We never let the strength of our faith go down just to make religion settle in more comfortably.

Faith = Expectancy

God does not answer some people's prayers because they never pray with faith. Our prayers have to be prayed by faith, and we must live lives of faith.

So many people don't know the difference between religion and spirituality. Religion has no expectancy. But the person who lives by faith radiates expectancy. You hear it in their voice; you see it in their countenance; you sense it in their presence.

> And Jesus answering saith unto them, Have faith in God. For verily I say unto you, That whosoever shall say unto this mountain, Be thou removed, and be thou cast into the sea; and shall not doubt in his heart, but shall believe that those things which he saith shall come to pass; he shall have whatsoever he saith (Mark 11:22-23).

A believer believes. It's the nature of a believer to believe. Let's go to another passage.

And [Jesus] did not [do] many mighty works there because of their unbelief (Matt. 13:58).

He did not do many mighty works because of their unbelief. Why don't we receive when we pray? Because we doubt. We don't have expectancy about it. We don't have faith.

The prayer of faith is prayed with confidence that God hears us. God's ears have not grown deaf over the ages. He does not need the Miracle Ear to hear His children. He hears us when we pray.

Childlike Faith

Somebody once asked me, "Why do we pray the way we pray?" Because God likes for kids to be kids. Don't you like your kids when they're being kids? They're just being themselves. No pretenses. They say what they feel, what they see, what they hear, what they believe. Do you see the simplicity of their belief?

You promise to take your little child somewhere, and he counts the days. "Daddy said we're going fishing on Saturday," little Johnny boasts to his friends. On Friday night, he can hardly sleep because he's so excited. Saturday morning comes, and he's up with the sun. You pull the pillow over your head and moan, "Can't I just sleep?"

"No, get up, Dad! You said, you said, you said."

See that belief? It has excitement to it. It has expectancy — like Christmas morning. The kid knocks the tree over to get that gift out from underneath it. That's expectancy.

That's what God desires our faith to be like. If we have the spirit of faith, that's what we will be like. We don't need to be mature and "deep in the Spirit" when we approach God. We should just be real. He's our Daddy. Jesus said if we don't have childlikeness, we can't enter into the kingdom of heaven (Luke 18:17).

Religion vs. True Spirituality

Romans 8:1 says: "There is therefore now no condemnation to them which are in Christ Jesus, who walk not after the flesh, but after the Spirit."

I like that word now. Religion is always in the past or way ahead in the future, but never in the present. It has no relevance to your life. So if your vocabulary is always "God did" and "God shall" but never "God is," there's something wrong. You've got too much religion in you.

Faith is a *now* expectancy. Hebrews 11:1 says, "Now faith is the substance of things hoped for, the evidence of things not seen." Anytime you're approaching God, you approach Him with an "is," not a "was" or a "going to be." God is a present-tense God. He will heal you now. He will deliver you now.

Religion has taken its toll upon the citizens of our nation and in many parts of the world. Most Christians live in this religious mind-set. Everything else in their life they want now, but not God. And the only thing that can really be now is God. God can heal you now, save you now, deliver you now, give you the answer to your problem now.

Paul wrote to the Romans, "There is therefore now no condemnation to them which are in Christ Jesus."

You see, God is not condemning you. Religion condemns you, but God sets you free. God might convict you, but He never condemns you. The Holy Spirit convicts but offers a way out to freedom. He will heal you, forgive you, set you free and put you back where you belong. Your condemnation was given to Christ on the cross; He was condemned in your stead.

Notice how Paul says "to them who are in Christ Jesus." These things that we live by cannot be partaken of unless you are in Christ Jesus. You can't have the now-ness of God unless you come into the knowledge of salvation.

Christ Jesus lives. That's why there's so much *now* in the Bible. If He were dead, there would not be so much *now* there. You can't be *now* unless you're alive. Buddha *was*. That's why he can't do anything. Mohammed *was*. But Jehovah is alive, and He *is*. He is *I AM*. Not I was, or I'm going to be. God is a now God.

Your God is alive. His Word is alive. That's why it's been the number-one best-selling book throughout world history. It's a living book. It speaks to us in the present.

Carnal Christians

The second part of Romans 8:1 deals with how we choose to live as Christians — whether we walk "after the flesh" or "after the Spirit."

You can be born again and live in carnality. You can be born again and live with unbelief dominating your life. Many Christians believe that Jesus is the Savior, but they have no faith for anything else. They believe He is the Savior, and thus they are born again. But they don't live victorious, overcoming lives.

You see, religion and unbelief are brothers. They live very close together. Unbelief helps defend religion, and religion helps defend unbelief. They work together. You can be in the kingdom of God and be carnal. There are whole churches that function on their new birth experience, and the rest of their lives are spent in unbelief.

Don't settle for that! We are called to be living stones built up into a spiritual house of worship.

As I stated earlier in this book, there are two realms that you are in contact with: the natural realm and the spiritual realm. You have to decide which one is going to dominate your life because one will be more dominant than the other. Either you'll live by your carnal nature, with a degree of spiritual understanding and a touch of God in your life once in a while, or you'll be a spiritual person whose spirit has dominance over the carnal nature.

Carnality and spirituality are facts of life. You'll not get rid of either one, but one will dominate the other. You have to decide which one you're going to live by. If you live by the things of the flesh, the natural laws of the universe will have power over you. They will influence your decisions; they will influence what you do; they will influence how you react to circumstances.

If you live by the flesh, and the New York Stock Exchange plummets, you're broke and have no hope. But if your faith is in God, you know that your future is in God's hands.

The supernatural is more powerful than the natural. Carnal law says, When cancer has you, you shall die. God's law says, No matter what it is, you can be healed and live in divine health.

Which principles are going to govern your life?

Remember that to walk after the Spirit instead of the flesh is a choice — not an anointing. Walking in the Spirit is a choice that brings greater opportunities and greater manifestations of God in your life. But many people — especially Pentecostals and charismatics — want an anointing first. That's why they can't live the Spirit life. They have it backward.

Carnal belief says, like Thomas, I'll only believe if I put my hands in His sides. If I see the holes in His hands, then I'll believe.

That's natural belief — being led by your senses. You can't live like that if you want to do great things for God. You have to live by what you know from the Word and from out of your spirit. But it's a choice you make. It's a great choice.

> There is therefore now no condemnation to them which are in Christ Jesus, who walk not after the flesh, but after the Spirit. For the law of the Spirit of life in Christ Jesus hath made me free from the law of sin and death.
>
> For what the law could not do, in that it was weak through the flesh, God sending his own Son in the likeness of sinful flesh, and for sin, condemned sin in the flesh: that the righteousness of the law might be fulfilled in us, who walk not after the flesh, but after the Spirit (Rom. 8:1-4).

The law of life in Christ Jesus sets us free from the law of sin and death. The sin nature is conquered by the born-again nature. It is crucified daily. The law of life kills the law of death — any degree of death that is in you.

Now notice that these things cannot come about unless you walk according to the Spirit life, according to the laws of the kingdom of God. All these principles, all these great truths cannot be partaken of by the carnal man. They are partaken of by your spirit, but it is faith that appropriates them in your life.

No Flakes, Please

Living in the Spirit does not mean you become weird. You simply become spiritually minded, but never religious-nut minded. Being spiritual, whether deep or shallow, is never weird, flaky or cornball-like. Spirituality is relatability. The more truly spiritual you are, the more relatable you should be. Remember that the next time somebody comes up to you and claims to be "deep in the Spirit," and you feel weird and want to run from them. It may be a good sign that it's the wrong spirit they're deep into. The Holy Spirit draws people. His presence attracts people. Spirituality is attractive when you live it in the right way.

The Rebel's Yell

One of the biggest strongholds of the carnal nature is the spirit of rebellion. Rebellion likes to have its own way. Rebellion cannot submit. It cannot flow. It has no joy unless it's fighting and exerting some type of power over people and events. The Bible calls it witchcraft (see 1 Sam. 15:23).

Rebellion says, I have a right to believe this or that, even when it's contradictory to the Word. I have a right to do this, even thought it goes against the flow of what God is doing.

Well, sure, you can do what you want and call it your right, but it's actually rebellion. Call it by its rightful name.

Rebellion is often disguised, and that makes it all the more creepy. Some Christians will never learn to walk in the Spirit because their rebellion will kill them first. And what is amazing to me is that they protect it.

What is the opposite of rebellion? Faith and submission to the Holy Spirit. And the greatest leaders, the greatest in the kingdom of God, are the ones most submitted to heaven.

NINE

WHY TONGUES?

We have examined the importance of faith in the life of a believer. But faith does you no good unless it is used. An arrow will never find its target without the propulsion of the bow wielded in the hand of the archer.

Faith is like an arrow: It must be fired off through the "bow" of prayer to be effective in your life. Prayer takes your faith and aims it toward heaven, fully expecting God's answer.

In this chapter I want to focus your attention on a

specialized type of prayer that is one of the mainstays of life in the Spirit: praying in tongues.

Why do we need to pray in tongues or pray in the Spirit? Aren't prayers that are uttered in a natural language good enough? God hears and answers your natural-language prayers, but He also has provided a supernatural form of prayer that transcends natural-language prayer.

Praying in the Spirit is not just something we do to set us apart as charismatics and Pentecostals. It is a scriptural way of praying with its own unique set of benefits for the believer.

With Signs Following

After Jesus issued the Great Commission to His disciples (see Mark 16:15), He told them what signs, or supernatural activities, would follow those who believed on Him. This is actually the second part of the Great Commission.

> He that believeth and is baptized shall be saved; but he that believeth not shall be damned. And these signs shall follow them that believe; in my name shall they cast out devils; they shall speak with new tongues (Mark 16:16-17).

Let's go to Acts 2 and take a refresher course on the purposes of praying in tongues.

> And when the day of Pentecost was fully come, they were all with one accord in one

place. And suddenly there came a sound from heaven as of a rushing mighty wind, and it filled all the house where they were sitting.

And there appeared unto them cloven tongues like as of fire, and it sat upon each of them. And they were all filled with the Holy Ghost, and began to speak with other tongues, as the Spirit gave them utterance (Acts 2:1-4).

The Bible says, "They were all filled with the Holy Ghost, *and....*" The word *and* is a conjunction; it means that whatever follows goes with whatever preceded it. "And they began to speak with other tongues."

I believe that some people who are filled with the Holy Spirit have not released the speaking in tongues part. This may be because of an absence of knowledge. But I believe that the full baptism of the Holy Spirit is always evidenced by speaking in tongues.

You'll see as we examine different portions of Scripture that this is true. But notice here that it says, "As the Spirit gave them utterance."

What does that mean? It means that where He lives in the innermost part of your being — in your spirit — from there rivers of living water will flow. Out of your spirit you'll begin to hear the voice of the Spirit giving you utterances. You'll hear it on the inside. But you have to open your mouth and speak it out.

No Need for Dramatics

When you receive the baptism in the Holy Spirit, there is no need for dramatic emotion or jerking or falling down. It's just like saying, "One, two, three," and you're off, speaking in tongues. What happens? I hear from inside, where the Holy Spirit speaks to my spirit.

Some people, when they first begin to speak in tongues, do not have fluency or a large spiritual vocabulary. They are like little children when they're first learning how to speak, talking in broken words as they're learning.

And in the Spirit life, newly Spirit-filled believers may have only one word or sound and just say it over and over. That's OK. It's part of growth and maturing. But your prayer language should grow. There should be more things coming up from your spirit as the Spirit of God gives you utterance.

You don't have to receive the baptism in an emotional frenzy. Nor should you get hung up on the "tarrying" doctrine. Some people tarry so long that they die without receiving the promise of the Spirit.

Believers tarried in the book of Acts because they were waiting for the coming of the Holy Spirit. Jesus told them to wait for the promise of the Father (see Acts 1:4). They were waiting for the coming of the Comforter. But now that we are living on this side of the event, there need not be any tarrying to receive the Holy Spirit, because He's come. Hallelujah, He's come.

Let's look again at our Scripture verse: "And they... began to speak with other tongues, as the Spirit gave them utterance" (Acts 2:4).

Does the Holy Spirit always want to pray in tongues through you? I believe He wants to pray through you and with you more often than most people think. Notice that every time you get in a place where you are hearing the Spirit, here comes that desire to pray. He inspires natural-language prayers and prayers in tongues. Any time you yield yourself to Him, He's ready to oblige that yielding with the utterance and the flow of God in your spirit.

So being filled with the Spirit is not just a one-time event to prove to you and your friends that you are filled with the Holy Spirit. The constant infilling of the Spirit keeps you full of the mighty power of the Holy Spirit. It's a continual experience.

Let's look at some other examples in the book of Acts.

> While Peter yet spake these words, the Holy Ghost fell on all them which heard the word (Acts 10:44).

Hearing the Word will cause the Holy Spirit to move. Notice the order of things in Scripture. It always says they heard the Word and were healed, or they heard the Word, and they got their answer. Here they heard the Word, and we'll see what happened next.

> And they of the circumcision which believed were astonished, as many as came with Peter, because that on the Gentiles also was poured out the gift of the Holy Ghost. For they heard them speak with tongues, and magnify God (Acts 10:45-46).

They received the Holy Spirit, and they spoke with tongues. Notice that the two go together.

The Bible says that "in the mouth of two or three

witnesses shall every word be established" (2 Cor. 13:1), so let's look at still another scripture.

> And it came to pass, that, while Apollos was at Corinth, Paul having passed through the upper coasts came to Ephesus: and finding certain disciples, he said unto them, Have ye received the Holy Ghost since ye believed? And they said unto him, We have not so much as heard whether there be any Holy Ghost.
>
> And he said unto them, Unto what then were ye baptized? And they said, Unto John's baptism. Then said Paul, John verily baptized with the baptism of repentance, saying unto the people, that they should believe on him which should come after him, that is, on Christ Jesus.
>
> When they heard this, they were baptized in the name of the Lord Jesus. And when Paul had laid his hands upon them, the Holy Ghost came on them; and they spake with tongues, and prophesied (Acts 19:1-6).

When Paul met these disciples, he said, "Have you received the Holy Ghost?"

It was important to Paul that the disciples he met were filled with the Holy Spirit. From the wording of Scripture we can tell it wasn't an afterthought, because the first thing he said to them was, "Have you received the Holy Ghost?"

They answered, "We don't even know whether there is a Holy Ghost."

That probably caught Paul off guard. He asked

them, "Well, then under what baptism are you baptized?"

And they replied, "John's baptism." They hadn't witnessed the upper room experience on the day of Pentecost, nor had they been around those who were there.

So Paul said, "Well, brothers, John truly baptized with the baptism of repentance, but you remember what John said — that you are to believe on the One that comes after him, and that One is Christ Jesus."

What did they do? They believed. Verse 5 says that when they heard this word, they were baptized in the name of the Lord Jesus. Paul laid his hands on them, and the Holy Spirit came on them. But notice: "The Holy Ghost came on them; and they spake with tongues, and prophesied."

These people not only received their prayer language, but they also started operating in the gift of prophecy. You see, being baptized in the Holy Spirit helps you flow in the gifts of the Holy Spirit.

So this is your third Scripture "witness": "The Holy Ghost came on them; and they spake with tongues, and prophesied." But I'm not finished. I have some more witnesses for you.

Turn back a couple of chapters to Acts 9, where we find the story of Paul's conversion. At this point he was still known as Saul of Tarsus — a fearless persecutor of the church. He's been knocked off his horse, stricken blind and had a vision, all at the same instant.

> And Saul arose from the earth; and when his eyes were opened, he saw no man: but they led him by the hand, and brought him into

Damascus. And he was three days without sight, and neither did eat nor drink (Acts 9:8-9).

I don't think I would eat or drink either. Just imagine this poor man's shock factor. One minute he's on his horse going to the next city and looking for Christians to persecute, then, *bam*, he's knocked off his horse, wakes up out of a vision and can't see.

This great man, whom all the Christians feared, had to be taken by the hand and led into Damascus. And for three days and nights, what did he do? Let's read on to find out.

And there was a certain disciple at Damascus, named Ananias; and to him said the Lord in a vision, Ananias. And he said, Behold, I am here, Lord.

And the Lord said unto him, Arise, and go into the street which is called Straight, and inquire in the house of Judas for one called Saul, of Tarsus:

For, behold, he prayeth (Acts 9:10-11).

Remember that this is the guy who stood by and watched Stephen be murdered. This is the man who incited fear among believers wherever he went. Now he's praying and fasting with everything he has. Let's pick up the story again.

[Paul] hath seen in a vision a man named Ananias coming in, and putting his hand on him, that he might receive his sight.

Then Ananias answered, Lord, I have heard by many of this man, how much evil he hath done to thy saints at Jerusalem: And here he hath authority from the chief priests to bind all that call on thy name.

But the Lord said unto him, Go thy way: for he is a chosen vessel unto me, to bear my name before the Gentiles, and kings, and the children of Israel: For I will shew him how great things he must suffer for my name's sake.

And Ananias went his way, and entered into the house; and putting his hands on him said, Brother Saul, the Lord, even Jesus, that appeared unto thee in the way as thou camest, hath sent me, that thou mightest receive thy sight, and be filled with the Holy Ghost.

And immediately there fell from his eyes as it had been scales: and he received sight forthwith, and arose, and was baptized (Acts 9:12-18).

Because this verse does not actually state that Paul spoke in tongues, some people use it to validate their not speaking in tongues when they are baptized in the Holy Spirit. Paul wrote more about tongues than anybody else in the Bible. He also wrote:

I thank my God, I speak with tongues more than ye all (1 Cor. 14:18).

I believe he did speak with tongues when he received the Holy Spirit. It's just not recorded in black and white in Scripture. Why would the Holy Spirit be different with Paul's infilling than He was with all the other infillings we read about?

Now let me give you some reasons for praying in tongues so that you're not just doing it without scriptural reasons. There are several reasons for praying in tongues.

- Praying in tongues edifies you or builds you up spiritually. Look what Paul wrote to the Corinthians.

He that speaketh in an unknown tongue edifieth himself (1 Cor. 14:4).

By praying in tongues we are built up to carry out the works of God in our time. Praying in tongues strengthens your spirit.

If you have a wimpy spirit, it may be because you're not praying in tongues enough. I want to balance that by saying your Word level is very important to your spiritual growth and strength — hearing the Word, reading the Word, praying the Word, confessing the Word. But don't neglect praying in tongues.

Is it possible to pray in tongues too much?

No! You cannot overdose on tongues. Of course, you need to pray in English, but you can also pray in tongues alongside it or alternate back and forth.

Never underestimate the importance of praying in tongues. It makes your spirit strong.

Remember that TV commercial years ago about Hefty trashbags? It was either wimpy, wimpy or Hefty, Hefty. You have to decide what kind of container you want to be, a wimpy one or a hefty, two-ply one. I want to be a hefty, two-ply container that can hold a lot of God's mighty power. What about you?

Where do you pray in tongues for edification? Do you have to be in your prayer closet to pray that way? No, you can pray in tongues while you're driving your car. You can do it while you're washing dishes, cleaning the house or mowing the lawn.

Do you have to pray loud?

No. I emphasize praying strong; and when you do pray strong there's usually a greater degree of volume. But I'm not trying to propagate a yelling contest.

As a child I was taught by Grandma to pray loud enough for my ears to hear my voice, and to me that is still a good balance. But be considerate of the environment you're in.

- Speaking in tongues reminds us of the Holy Spirit's residence within us. Jesus told us:

I will pray the Father, and he shall give you another Comforter, that he may abide with you for ever; even the Spirit of truth; whom the world cannot receive, because it seeth him not, neither knoweth him: but ye know him; for he dwelleth with you, and shall be in you (John 14:16-17).

- Praying in tongues helps us pray correctly.

Likewise the Spirit also helpeth our infirmities: for we know not what we should pray for as we ought: but the Spirit itself maketh intercession for us with groanings which cannot be uttered.

And he that searcheth the hearts knoweth what is the mind of the Spirit, because he maketh intercession for the saints according to the will of God (Rom. 8:26-27).

When we don't know how to pray, we can always trust the Holy Spirit to pray through us, in tongues, exactly what needs to be prayed.

Sometimes people come up and ask me if I will pray for them about something. I usually don't know their particular situation. But I know I want God to help them, so I say, "Father, I lift them up to you," and I just start praying in the Spirit and let the Holy Spirit pray through me. That way I'm praying correctly for their specific situation.

- Praying in tongues stimulates our faith.

But ye, beloved, [build] up yourselves on your most holy faith, [by] praying in the Holy Ghost (Jude 20).

- Praying in tongues helps keep us from foul talk.

Praying in the Spirit helps tame this unruly member of our body called the tongue. If we yield our tongue, our voice and our speech to the Holy Spirit, we will avoid worldly contamination.

- Praying in tongues brings spiritual refreshing. Jesus said:

He that believeth on me, as the scripture hath said, out of his belly shall flow rivers of living water. (But this spake he of the Spirit, which they that believe on him should receive: for the Holy Ghost was not yet given; because that Jesus was not yet glorified) (John 7:38-39).

As the Holy Spirit flows through us like rivers of living water, we are cleansed, refreshed and restored.

The great healing evangelist Smith Wigglesworth was once asked, "Why don't you take a vacation?"

He said, "I do take one," and he started praying in tongues. "That's the way I get my rest and my refreshing."

There is no rest for your spirit like praying in the Holy Spirit. He brings a refreshing to your spirit and to your soul. So if you're tired, you need to pray in tongues and get refreshed on the inside.

- Speaking in tongues helps build a sensitivity to the Holy Spirit.

By speaking in tongues regularly, you fine-tune your spirit's awareness of the Holy Spirit's indwelling presence.

For as many as are led by the Spirit of God, they are the sons of God. For ye have not received the spirit of bondage again to fear; but ye have received the Spirit of adoption, whereby we cry, Abba, Father. The Spirit itself beareth witness with our spirit, that we are the children of God (Rom. 8:14-16).

- Speaking in tongues gives us power to be witnesses.

But ye shall receive power, after that the Holy Ghost is come upon you: and ye shall be witnesses unto me both in Jerusalem, and in all Judea, and in Samaria, and unto the uttermost part of the earth (Acts 1:8).

Consider the transformation of the disciples after what happened on the day of Pentecost (Acts 2). These men, who formerly had doubted Jesus, denied Him, feared the masses and bickered among themselves over who was the greatest, suddenly were preaching with such boldness that the Bible says they turned the world upside down.

After Peter preached on the day of Pentecost, the Bible says three thousand people were added to the church that very day. That's powerful witnessing!

Enlisted for Battle

With that supernatural power to be witnesses for Christ comes automatic assault by the enemy. The devil doesn't like powerful Christians — those who know where they stand in Christ. He will do everything in his power to weaken and, if possible, even destroy them.

But, as we will see in the next chapter, the devil is no match for a believer who walks in the Spirit.

TEN

CONFRONTING DEVILS

Everyone who is led by the Spirit will find that demonic assault comes with the territory. You can't live in the realm of the Spirit without encountering devils, so you'd better learn how to fight them.

Paul told us:

> For we wrestle not against flesh and blood, but against principalities, against powers, against the rulers of the darkness of this

world, against spiritual wickedness in high places (Eph. 6:12).

These are your enemies: princes and rulers in the demonic realm. Paul told the Corinthians that he fought with "beasts" at Ephesus (see 1 Cor. 15:32). He wasn't talking about natural beasts like lions and tigers and bears. He was referring to spiritual beasts — principalities and powers over Ephesus.

As we get closer to the coming of the Lord, spiritual warfare is going to intensify. We are not called to fight a minor battle. We are called to fight major battles. If you seek to walk in the Spirit, you won't have to invite clashes with the enemy — they'll come looking for you. Get ready for seasons of warfare in the Christian life.

A Warning

Before we talk about confronting devils, let me give you this word of caution: Anybody who enters the world of the spirit without the Holy Spirit is a spiritualist — one who operates totally for self-gain or for the satanic world.

The only way a Christian can move into the spirit realm successfully and do things the way God wants them done is with the accompaniment of the Holy Spirit. He is your teacher, your guide. You never get to the place where you can enter the world of the spirit by yourself, without Him.

It's possible to project your spirit out there without the Holy Spirit. But it's real out there. Things happen when you get out there. So please, believers, stay with the Holy Spirit.

Operation Warfare

Before Jesus was taken back to heaven, He said the following words to the eleven disciples: "Go ye into all the world, and preach the gospel to every creature" (Mark 16:15). This famous mandate is what we call the Great Commission, but it was really more like a command. I like to call it the Great Command.

But listen to what He says next.

> And these signs shall follow them that believe; In my name shall they cast out devils; they shall speak with new tongues; they shall take up serpents; and if they drink any deadly thing, it shall not hurt them; they shall lay hands on the sick, and they shall recover (vv. 17-18, italics added).

The very first thing Jesus said His followers would do is cast out devils. Then He said they would speak with tongues. Notice that these two almost always go together. We'll get to praying in tongues in the next chapter. Right now let's take a good look at how we drive out demons.

Now if we are called to war in the Spirit, then we are soldiers or warriors in God's kingdom. Paul tells us how we go about doing this supernatural task:

> For though we walk in the flesh, we do not war after the flesh: (For the weapons of our warfare are not carnal, but mighty through God to the pulling down of strong holds;) casting down imaginations, and every high

thing that exalteth itself against the knowledge of God (2 Cor. 10:3-5).

Armed and Dangerous

No earthly soldier in his right mind would advance into enemy territory without the proper weapons and equipment. Neither should we as spiritual soldiers. God makes sure His warriors have everything they need to wipe out the enemy. But it's up to us to put our spiritual armor on. Listen to how Paul describes it.

> Wherefore take unto you the whole armour of God, that ye may be able to withstand in the evil day, and having done all, to stand. Stand therefore, having your loins girt about with truth, and having on the breastplate of righteousness; and your feet shod with the preparation of the gospel of peace; above all, taking the shield of faith, wherewith ye shall be able to quench all the fiery darts of the wicked.
>
> And take the helmet of salvation, and the sword of the Spirit, which is the word of God: *praying always with all prayer and supplication in the Spirit,* and watching thereunto with all perseverance and supplication for all saints (Eph. 6:13-18, italics added).

With Spirit Power

I hope you noticed the ten words that sum up our entire strategy in clashing with demons: *"Praying always with all prayer and supplication in the Spirit.*"

You must be operating in the power of the Spirit. You see, God not only gave us our six pieces of armor, but He also gave us the most awesome piece of equipment any spiritual warrior could ever need: the power of the Holy Spirit.

Jesus had it.

> God anointed Jesus of Nazareth with the Holy Ghost and with power (Acts 10:38).

We have to have it too. Every true soldier must be anointed with the Holy Spirit's power. You can't fight devils with natural human might. It won't work, so don't even try it. You'll just make a fool of yourself and get all beat up.

The story of Paul and Silas in Philippi is one of the best accounts in the Bible of how to war against devils in the power of the Holy Spirit.

> And it came to pass, as we went to prayer, a certain damsel possessed with a spirit of divination met us, which brought her masters much gain by soothsaying:
>
> The same followed Paul and us, and cried, saying, These men are the servants of the most high God, which shew unto us the way of salvation. And this did she many days. But Paul, being grieved, turned and said to the spirit (Acts 16:16-18).

Being grieved in your spirit is usually the first signal that something is wrong. It doesn't necessarily mean there's something wrong with you. It just means that something in the atmosphere is wrong — *it means there is an attack.*

Just because you're jumping for joy now doesn't mean you won't have war tomorrow. But when your spirit grieves, you know you are about to hit a battle. That is not a cause for fear; it's a warning from headquarters to prepare. Pick up your armor, make sure it's all properly tuned and in place. Get ready to fight.

Notice that Paul "turned and said to the spirit." Remember, it's not flesh and blood but principalities and powers and princes that we war against. That's why I told you in chapter seven, "Don't touch things in the natural. Touch them in the Spirit where the real problem is."

That's what Paul did. He didn't talk to the girl or sit down and have a committee meeting to find out where her doctrine was wrong. He waited until the Holy Spirit moved upon him, and then he spoke.

> [Paul] turned and said to the spirit, I command thee in the name of Jesus Christ to come out of her. And he came out the same hour.
>
> And when her masters saw that the hope of their gains was gone, they caught Paul and Silas, and drew them into the marketplace unto the rulers, and brought them to the magistrates, saying, These men, being Jews, do exceedingly trouble our city (vv. 18-20).

When you fight devils, you stir up trouble. But, hallelujah, you also get free! You find liberty. That's what God wants you to walk in — liberty of the Spirit. When devils bother you, be like Paul. Turn and say, "You foul spirit, come out in the name of Jesus."

Spiritual Breakthrough

The rulers in Philippi thought that Paul and Silas "troubled the city" because they were Jews. But the real reason was because they were full of Holy Spirit power and faith to do signs and wonders!

And the multitude rose up together against them: and the magistrates rent off their clothes, and commanded to beat them. And when they had laid many stripes upon them, they cast them into prison, charging the jailor to keep them safely: Who, having received such a charge, thrust them into the inner prison, and made their feet fast in the stocks. And at midnight Paul and Silas prayed, and sang praises unto God: and the prisoners heard them.

And suddenly there was a great earthquake, so that the foundations of the prison were shaken: and immediately all the doors were opened, and every one's bands were loosed.

And the keeper of the prison awaking out of his sleep, and seeing the prison doors open, he drew out his sword, and would have killed himself, supposing that the prisoners had been fled.

But Paul cried with a loud voice, saying,

Do thyself no harm: for we are all here. Then he called for a light, and sprang in, and came trembling, and fell down before Paul and Silas, and brought them out, and said, Sirs, what must I do to be saved?

And they said, Believe on the Lord Jesus Christ, and thou shalt be saved, and thy house. And they spake unto him the word of the Lord, and to all that were in his house (Acts 16:22-32).

Counterattack

When the devil takes a blow, he always plans a counterattack. It won't always come back in the same way. It usually comes down other avenues. The counterattack on Paul and Silas didn't come through the possessed girl. It came through her masters — or rather through the devils controlling them. The girl's masters said, "These men touble our city," and they had Paul and Silas thrown in prison. Those devils thought they were rid of them.

But I tell you one thing: If you are a soldier of God, you will never be left in the enemy's prison camp. God will send angels to deliver you. But you must learn to rejoice and look to God while you are there.

What did Paul and Silas do? At the midnight hour they sang praises to God, and the prisoners heard them. They worshipped God. That's a weapon, people. You can pray in tongues, but you also have to worship God.

You see, when you worhip God, you give Him place and not the devil. When you worship God, the devil has to flee because God said that He inhabits the praises of His people. When God shows up, devils depart. When light comes, darkness goes.

Final Victory

Paul and Silas worshipped God. And God's glory touched the earth, shook that prison and those shackles fell off. The prison warden wanted to kill himself. But again Paul was led by the Spirit. "Paul cried with a loud voice, saying, Do thyself no harm: for we are all here" (v. 28).

When the jailer came, what was his first statement? "What must I do to be saved?"

The devil tried to kick these two men out of the city without winning a soul, without having an influence for God. But Paul troubled the city and preached everywhere, stirring up devils. He didn't just go and say, "Isn't God sweet?"

What a story! What people we have here! Paul went into the city and opened up his spirit and began to soar with God. If Paul were alive today, he would be called the most radical man on earth. But we are to be the most radical people on earth.

When the Philippian jailer fell at Paul's feet and cried, "What must I do to be saved?" Paul replied, "Believe on the Lord Jesus Christ, and thou shalt be saved, and thy house" (vv. 30-31).

Jesus Christ made a way so that not one of you should go down in defeat. No matter what battle you face — whether it is finances, sickness, rebellion in your children or spiritual backsliding — He made a way for you to win.

It's time we learned how to war on behalf of brothers and sisters in the body of Christ as well as for ourselves. The church must come to the point where believers all over the world will pull out their swords at the same time and go out against the powers of darkness.

That's the way families are supposed to work too. When the devil fights one member of the family, the others are supposed to join together and get on their knees and get in the Spirit and bombard the devil with Holy Spirit firepower. That's one of the biggest secrets to a happy home. The man of the house especially needs to learn it.

We are not in an imaginary world. The world of the Spirit is very real. A person who obeys God will confront devils many times. It comes with the territory. But remember that the Greater One lives inside of you. You are more than a conqueror through Christ. Let the devil know it by hitting him with your power. Quit being nice to him. Get him off your block, not just out of your house. War against him.

ELEVEN

SEVEN WAYS
GOD LEADS YOU

Throughout this book we've been learning about our nature as tripartite beings and God's desire that we be led by His Spirit. But how are we actually led by the Spirit of God? How can we know it's Him speaking to us?

I have identified seven different ways by which the Holy Spirit leads you.

The inward witness.

This is the number-one way that the Holy Spirit

leads His people. It can manifest as a check in your spirit or as a go-ahead sign. A security, a sense of strength and approval, a gladness, an inner feeling of victory — all of these have to do with the inward witness.

Sometimes people reach inside and all they feel is the pizza they ate last night, and that's not the Holy Spirit. Go a little bit deeper in there, and you will find the Spirit. But keep in mind that these feelings are different from the emotions of your soul. An inward witness will bring your emotions under God's control.

The inward witness is also probably the most familiar type of "leading." It's something all Christians can identify with, but perhaps not all of them recognize it for what it is. Sometimes inside you just feel like something is not right, and you have to wait for a go-ahead signal before proceeding.

Maybe when you began, your motivation was right, but somewhere along the line a problem cropped up. It could be an inward problem, a decision problem or something you cannot foresee. But God foresees it and says to wait. He tries to work on the other people involved or on yourself. If it doesn't work out, then His answer is no.

God tries to forewarn you, but not because He doesn't love the other person. He's dealing with that person too. God never deals with one and not the other.

Some people hear His voice better than others. And sometimes when people are in the wrong they don't want to hear what God is saying. So they shut their ears and gather to themselves people who agree with them, or people who are too weak to say no to their face.

The inward voice.

Sometimes on the inside you hear the voice of your spirit. This is not the same as the inward witness. This is a voice — the inward voice of your spirit. It is also called the conscience. The conscience is something built into every human spirit to help the individual discern right from wrong.

Paul wrote to the church at Rome:

> Which shew the work of the law written in their hearts, their conscience also bearing witness (Rom. 2:15).

And again,

> I say the truth in Christ, I lie not, my conscience also bearing me witness in the Holy Ghost (Rom. 9:1).

But the conscience can become "seared," or dulled, over time if we continually ignore it (see 1 Tim. 4:1-2). How can it be quickened once again? The answer is found in Hebrews.

> How much more shall the blood of Christ, who through the eternal Spirit offered himself without spot to God, purge your conscience from dead works to serve the living God? (Heb. 9:14).

The voice of the Holy Spirit.

How many of you have ever heard the still small voice on the inside? That's the Spirit of God speaking to your spirit. Listen to it. It's not voices — it's *His* voice filtered through your spirit. There is a difference between voices and His voice. His voice comes inside and always lines up with what is written in the Word.

First John 5:7 says, "For there are three that bear record in heaven, the Father, the Word, and the Holy Ghost: and these three are one."

Whatever comes in from the Spirit can be found in the Word. What you find in the Word will be found in spiritual manifestation. They go together. If the message you are receiving on the inside doesn't line up with the Word, then something is wrong. Don't make a move until you get God's mind on the matter.

It's better to be a little bit slow than too fast. At least you can speed up later. Sometimes, if you've gone too fast, you've already messed up so many things that it takes God five hundred miracles to get the situation back where it belongs.

If you have built sensitivity into your spirit by the Word and by prayer and by protection from worldly contamination, you can get so tuned in to the Spirit's voice that it sounds audible.

This is why some folks say they have heard the voice of God audibly. Now God does speak audibly at times. I can't say He doesn't because the Bible says He does. But He speaks on the inside more than He speaks on the outside. And if you build enough sensitivity, when He does speak through your spirit it sounds so loud on the inside that you think it's audible.

Acts 10 records the story of Peter's vision concerning the Gentiles.

> While Peter thought on the vision, the Spirit said unto him, Behold, three men seek thee. Arise therefore, and get thee down, and go with them, doubting nothing: for I have sent them.
>
> Then Peter went down to the men which were sent unto him from Cornelius; and said, Behold, I am he whom you seek: what is the cause wherefore ye are come?
>
> And they said, Cornelius the centurion, a just man, and one that feareth God, and of good report among all the nation of the Jews, was warned from God by an holy angel to send for thee into his house, and to hear words of thee.
>
> Then called he them in, and lodged them. Then on the morrow Peter went away with them, and certain brethren from Joppa accompanied him (vv. 19-23).

Notice in verse 19 it says, "While Peter thought on the vision."

Remember the vision about the sheet with all the unclean creatures in it? He was thinking about it. And "the Spirit said unto him" (v. 19).

There is a difference between your spirit speaking and the Spirit of God speaking. With practice, and over a period of seasoning, you can distinguish between the two. Now the Holy Spirit is always in there. He can unction my spirit to say things, and because

I've fed my spirit on the Word, it will speak. But there are times when the Spirit of God will speak.

While Peter thought about the vision, the Holy Spirit said to him, "Three men seek thee...go with them, doubting nothing." In other words, "Don't worry. But make sure you get this one thing, Peter — *go with them.*"

That is how the Spirit of God speaks to you.

Remember the story of Samuel?

> And it came to pass at that time, when Eli was laid down in his place,...and Samuel was laid down to sleep; that the Lord called Samuel: and he answered, Here am I (1 Sam. 3:2-4).

Eli had already gone to bed. Samuel had just gotten into bed, and the Spirit of God said, "Samuel, Samuel." Three times Samuel went to Eli, and finally Eli figured out that God had come back to the temple to say something.

Now let's return to the book of Acts.

> Now there were in the church that was at Antioch certain prophets and teachers....As they ministered to the Lord, and fasted, the Holy Ghost said, Separate me Barnabas and Saul for the work whereunto I have called them. And when they had fasted and prayed, and laid their hands on them, they sent them away (Acts 13:1-3).

Notice here too that as the people in the church at

Antioch ministered to the Lord, and fasted and prayed, the Holy Spirit said. Now, what's the difference between your spirit's voice being unctioned by the Holy Spirit and the Holy Spirit speaking directly to you?

First, the voice sounds different. The Holy Spirit's voice has more authority to it than the voice of your spirit. That's how I always tell the difference — one has more authority than the other.

So this is another way the Spirit of God leads us today — by speaking to us directly.

Knowings.

Isn't it funny how sometimes you just know something? You don't know why you know, but you just know? This is another way you can be led by the Spirit — you just have a knowing. Did you ever get a knowing but didn't follow it, and later you were in trouble? You said, "How did I get in this mess?" Well, for about two days you had a knowing that you didn't investigate. Then later you paid for it.

Investigate your knowings. Run from your wonderings. Most of the time we investigate our wonderings and run from our knowings. We wonder if there is more out there. And we don't investigate that absolute knowing inside.

God leads us by knowings. This can also be through the inward witness, but I like to put it in a separate category because it can be so strong. You just know.

That knowing inside comes from the Spirit of God. You see, when God speaks to you, He just comes down and puts it inside you. He doesn't always give you the reasons why a thing is right. You may not

119

discover the reasons until after the fact.

Remember Agent 007? He wanted to know all the information up front, and his boss would say, "All information will be given on a need-to-know basis." Sometimes that's how the Spirit of God is — He tells us things on a need-to-know basis.

I used to have trouble with that. I thought, "I have to have some kind of proof to make this right." The proof always came after the fact. If I didn't follow the knowing, I got in trouble. I've learned to follow my knowings more by the mistakes — by missing them — than by being deeper in the Spirit.

After a while I learned that every time I override this thing I get in trouble. Every time I override it I have to go back and fix something. It's just that way. Trust God and follow it.

Occasionally we get the whole picture. Most of the time we get it in parts. If God gave you everything up front, you wouldn't have to walk by faith. You would not need to trust Him. God operates by faith. He would never do anything to undermine your faith in Him.

Visions.

One of the characteristics of the end times is that visions are to increase. In Acts 2 Peter quoted from Joel's prophecy:

> And it shall come to pass in the last days, saith God, I will pour out of my Spirit upon all flesh: and your sons and your daughters shall prophesy, and your young men shall see visions, and your old men shall dream dreams (v. 17).

There are five different kinds of visions. Let's take a look at each of them.

The inward vision. By definition this kind of vision occurs when you see something on the inside. Remember the inward witness and the inward voice? Well, now we have the inward eye. Perhaps there have been times in your life when you've "seen" something or had a picture of something on the inside. That's called an inward vision.

Most folks have had this kind of vision but didn't know it was a vision. You hear inwardly, you have feelings inwardly, yet you can also see inwardly. And when people say they've had a vision, it's usually because of what they have seen on the inside.

But oftentimes people want dramatics — lightning crashing, a cloud rolling across the room and then some strange images projected on the wall.

The inward vision is the most common type of vision of the New Testament. What you see, you see on the inside. God shows you something. Sometimes it is in color; sometimes it is in black and white. Sometimes there is sound; sometimes there is not. Sometimes you just see and then God gives you the interpretation later. Other times you just act out what you saw in the vision.

The trance. The trance is probably the least common type of vision, but it does occur.

> On the morrow, as they went on their journey, and drew nigh unto the city, Peter went up upon the housetop to pray about the sixth hour: And he became very hungry, and would have eaten: but while

they made ready, he fell into a trance (Acts
10:9-10).

Trances are rare, but they are biblical. What does a
trance do?

A trance suspends all of your physical senses and
activities. It's like a frozen state where you are more
aware of the spiritual realm, and what you are seeing
and feeling there, than of the natural realm.

When a person falls into a trance their physical
body is almost paralyzed while they are out in the
Spirit and being shown something.

Here Peter was praying on the rooftop. He probably
went up there just to be alone with the Lord and to
inquire of heaven. While he was up there the Spirit of
God fell upon him and put him into a trance.

It was during this trance — which is a type of vision
— that Peter saw the sheet with all the "unclean" creatures in it. Through this vision Peter received revelation that God intended to save the "unclean" gentiles
also.

He told the centurion Cornelius, "But God hath
shewed me that I should not call any man common or
unclean" (Acts 10:28).

The open vision. The open vision is when, for example, I am talking to you and, as I am, God opens up
my eyes to see something in the Spirit. You don't even
know I am seeing something. I hear myself talking,
but it's as if my voice is coming from a great distance.
All the while my eyes are looking at something else.

In the open vision, you could be walking down a
corridor in a busy airport, but you don't bump into
anyone. Nothing happens. You are not aware of what

is in front of you or beside you, but you just keep right on walking. Meanwhile you are seeing and hearing something in the spirit realm.

Let me stop to make this point: God never shows you something for your entertainment. Everything comes for a purpose. There is no such thing as a view of something just for the sake of having a vision — that's a religious devil accommodating your desire for the dramatic, or it's a false spirit. God never does anything without a significant purpose.

Night vision or dream. The distinguishing mark of a night vision is that it is a God-given dream. Remember the story of Joseph in the New Testament? While he was asleep, the angel of the Lord appeared to him in a dream and told him to flee into Egypt with Mary and the child Jesus to thwart King Herod's attempt on His life (see Matt. 2:13).

That came in a dream. You'll notice in the life of Joseph that that's the way he was mainly led. Every time God spoke to Joseph it was in a dream. Mary had more of an open vision (see Luke 1:26-38).

I don't know why some people are given more to certain things than others. Bob may be led mainly through the inward voice, while Sue has God-given dreams. Perhaps you have neither, but you frequently have unexplainable knowings.

All I can tell you is that God is sovereign and deals with each one differently. However God deals with you, be confident that He does deal with you, and rejoice in it.

"But I want to have more visions."

Well, don't look at me. It's not scriptural to seek them. If you do seek visions, you will get the fifth kind — the false vision.

False visions. A false vision is a counterfeit of any of the legitimate, biblical forms of visions we just covered. Evil spirits do accommodate people with false visions. I classify some of these false visions as vain imaginations, which are usually produced by the soul. The soul will produce a religious vision to see if you will yield to it. You have to keep your soul in check and judge the vision by the Word and deal with it.

So the soul can generate false visions, or vain imaginations, but there are also demonic visions masquerading as true spiritual visions.

A demonic vision usually has tragedy, error or mischievousness in it. You can discern their origin by the character of them.

When God shows you danger, He does it in a sense of warning — not a sense of fright. You may feel the gravity of what you see, but you will never be left without the sense of His security, His peace, over the whole situation.

The Word.

God leads us by His Word. When all your senses fail and all your sights dry up, you aren't left out in the cold. You have sixty-six books that tell you what to do.

Everything we see, hear, perceive — all these things must be in line with the Word. God does not speak beyond His written Word. You should never go beyond the Word.

Get free according to the Word. Get free in line with the Word. Get free with what the Word says.

Paul told Timothy, "Timothy, my son, keep sound

doctrine. Hold fast to sound doctrine. Don't let go of good doctrine and a good conscience and right thinking."

Judge what I say by the Word. Judge what I do by the Word. If it's not in line with the Word, get rid of it.

Prophecy.

The seventh way God leads His people is through the gift of the Spirit called prophecy.

Now before we talk about the place of prophecy in the Spirit's leading, let me issue a warning: Be careful about your relationship to the gift of prophecy and especially the whole domain of personal prophecy. I'll elaborate on this in chapter eleven.

I'm not suggesting you excommunicate it from your life but that you simply put it in its rightful position. I say this in reaction to the excessive dependence upon prophecy that we see today.

God does speak through prophets, but more often He will speak directly to your spirit in one of the five ways we've just discussed. I'd rather hear God for myself any day than rely on Prophet Joe to tell me what God has for my life.

Prophecy, like visions, is also something you should not seek. It has its place in the Christian's life. But when your life is dependent upon it, something is wrong.

When a church feels that it has not had a good service unless somebody has prophesied outright through tongues and interpretation, it means something is out of whack.

If it never occurs, then there is a problem too. But if prophecy is always a dominant factor, where everybody gauges the success of a service or conference by how many prophecies there were and who said what, then there is a problem.

With that said, let me state that prophecy is a New Testament fact, and we have Scripture verses to prove its legitimacy for the church. We'll dig into the meat of it in the next chapter.

TWELVE

UNDERSTANDING THE PROPHETIC

Many Christians think prophecy only pertains to the telling of the future. But that's not what the Bible says: "But he that prophesieth speaketh unto men to edification, and exhortation, and comfort " (1 Cor. 14:3). The purpose of prophecy is to build up, encourage (exhort) and comfort the church and individual believers. If you think prophecy is just the telling of futuristic events, you are missing the whole New Testament teaching on prophecy.

The story in Acts 21 is one I like to read whenever

I teach on the gift of prophecy.

> And the next day we that were of Paul's
> company departed, and came unto Caesarea:
> and we entered into the house of Philip the
> evangelist, which was one of the seven; and
> abode with him. And the same man had four
> daughters, virgins, which did prophesy.
>
> And as we tarried there many days, there
> came down from Judea a certain prophet,
> named Agabus. And when he was come in
> unto us, he took Paul's girdle, and bound his
> own hands and feet, and said, Thus saith the
> Holy Ghost, So shall the Jews at Jerusalem
> bind the man that owneth this girdle, and
> shall deliver him into the hands of the Gen-
> tiles. And when we heard these things, both
> we, and they of that place, besought him not
> to go up to Jerusalem.
>
> Then Paul answered, What mean ye to
> weep and to break mine heart? for I am ready
> not to be bound only, but also to die at
> Jerusalem for the name of the Lord Jesus.
> And when he would not be persuaded, we
> ceased, saying, The will of the Lord be done.
> And after those days we took up our car-
> riages, and went up to Jerusalem (Acts 21:8-15).

This story contains a personal prophecy relating to
Paul. We can draw from it several different facts: 1) It
is a New Testament occurrence; 2) it is scriptural; 3) it
is for today. But we must be careful to place it correctly in our lives.

Verse 10 says that a certain prophet named Agabus came, and notice that with the prophetic word came a demonstration or a symbolic action. Agabus took Paul's girdle and bound his own hands and feet. It proves God likes drama.

> When he was come unto us, he took Paul's girdle, and bound his own hands and feet, and said, Thus saith the Holy Ghost (v. 11).

By this symbolic action Agabus was saying that the man who owned the girdle would be bound and delivered into the hands of the gentiles. When everybody heard this prophecy, including the folks that were with Paul, they began to say, "Paul don't do this — don't go."

The problem was they had the wrong interpretation of God's speaking. That is the number-one difficulty with personal prophecy: not the issue of whether God has spoken legitimately but how people interpret it and try to place it in your life.

The Christians at Caesarea all said, "Paul, don't go!"

Paul said, "What is this? I'm willing not only to be bound but also to die for the Lord."

God was warning Paul of what was about to happen to him in Jerusalem and ultimately in Rome. We all know the story of the life of Paul, how he was bound in chains, survived a shipwreck and so forth. It was because God wanted to place him before the great leaders of that time period.

> The Lord stood by him, and said, Be of good cheer, Paul: for as thou hast testified of me in

Jerusalem, so must thou bear witness also at Rome (Acts 23:11).

God doesn't always promise to take you first-class. He just gets you there. Sometimes the way we choose to go and the way God chooses to go are two different routes. That's why Paul said he had learned to abound and to be abased.

And so his fellow disciples pleaded with him not to go to Jerusalem, but they could not persuade him. That shows the strength of character in Paul. When they realized he would not budge, they said, "Well, let the will of the Lord be done."

They should have said that in the first place. Why did they try to resist the prophecy? They loved Paul. They wanted him to be free and not in jail. But Paul knew that suffering was part of his calling. Remember what God told him when he was knocked off his horse? He was going to suffer many things. And God showed him then that many people would suffer for the name of Christ. Paul already knew this was a crucial part of his destiny.

The prophecy that came by Agabus was straightforward. Agabus didn't try to interpret it. Many times the person delivering the prophecy tries to interpret it instead of just delivering it. Don't speak any more than what God gives you, and don't try to speculate after it is over.

Sometimes when I give a word during a meeting, the person will come up to me afterward and say, "Well, do you have anything else for me?"

And I'll say, "No, I gave it to you. If I had something more that needed to be said, I would have told you to come up and see me afterward."

Many times God only gives me a prophecy in part. The other part may come some other way. If you don't fully understand, go seek it out and wait upon the Spirit of God and say, "God, help me to know this thing clearly. Help me with this. I need to hear from You."

Some things are not to be said publicly. Some things are to be said privately because they are nobody else's business. Sometimes when you speak prophetically you don't know what you are talking about. You just know it's the Holy Spirit, and you are delivering His message. And people act like you know their whole life history. All I know is what I said — I don't know the before or the after. And I really don't want to know — it's none of my business. I have enough going on in my life without figuring out yours.

This is where people get soulishly addicted to the prophetic and to those who operate easily in this gift. They want to be given a prophetic word instead of seeking God in His written Word.

But God does use personal prophecy — it just needs to be judged. If the prophecy you've received is not in line with the character of God and the Scriptures — don't heed it.

Some people are given more to the utterance gifts than others. If they can carry these gifts maturely and keep them in order, that's great. But God never intends for one person to have, say, the gift of prophecy "better" than others. It depends on the yieldedness of individuals and the choice of God — whom He chooses to flow through.

Sometimes when the gift of the Spirit comes into the

room — tongues and interpretation — I will know the whole prophecy before it is ever said. That way I can judge it to find out what is of God and what is just that person speaking. I'll know when they are supposed to stop.

Lester Sumrall tells a story of when he and Smith Wigglesworth were in a conference together. It was the first time he had met Wigglesworth.

Sumrall got up to preach, and he was preaching away and kept right on preaching. After a while Wigglesworth came up behind him, put his hand on his shoulder and said, "Son, it would have been wise for you to have ended fifteen minutes ago when the Holy Ghost ended." And he shut down the meeting.

So many people go beyond the Holy Spirit. Sometimes a prophecy is short, and sometimes it is lengthy. You can discern with your spiritual ears when a person goes into the realm of their own human spirit.

One just starting out in the gift of prophecy will go back and forth because they don't know better. They're learning, and there is grace for that. But there are some who will prophesy and just keep right on going. You have to say, "Stop right there."

Sometimes the interpretation is longer or shorter than the tongue. It's like when I preach in Germany or Russia. When I say, "Hello," there may be a longer way of saying hello in that language, and I'll have to wait for the interpreter to finish.

There is that difference in the realm of the Spirit too. You cannot always judge by the length of a tongue how long its interpretation will be.

If you are a leader, you should develop your spirit and fine-tune your sensitivity to the point that you always know what is going on in your church. Paul warned us about what can happen if the utterance gifts get out of control.

Sounding Brass, Clanging Cymbals

Paul had to correct the church at Corinth for their disorderly services.

> How is it then, brethren? when ye come together, every one of you hath a psalm, hath a doctrine, hath a tongue, hath a revelation, hath an interpretation. Let all things be done unto edifying (1 Cor. 14:26).

Here we have a group of people who were way out of order. Everybody was in competition to be the most spiritual. Paul had to set them straight. Earlier in this same letter he told them that even if they spoke "with the tongues of men and of angels" but had no love motivating them, they were nothing more than "sounding brass" and "clanging cymbals" (1 Cor. 13:1, NKJV). In other words, nothing but noise.

Next he addressed specifically the utterance gifts — *tongues, interpretation* and *prophecy.*

> If any man speak in an unknown tongue, let it be by two, or at the most by three, and that by course; and let one interpret. But if there be no interpreter, let him keep silence in the church; and let him speak to himself, and to God.
>
> Let the prophets speak two or three, and

let the other judge. For ye may all prophesy one by one, that all may learn, and all may be comforted. For God is not the author of confusion, but of peace, as in all churches of the saints (vv. 27-33).

Why Do We Need to Interpret?

Notice the importance Paul places on interpretation: "If there be no interpreter, let him keep silence" (v. 28). Why is it so important to interpret a word given in tongues?

I would that ye all spake with tongues, but rather that ye prophesied: for greater is he that prophesieth than he that speaketh with tongues, except he interpret, that the church may receive edifying (1 Cor. 14:5).

That's the bottom line — that the church, the body of Christ, be edified, or built up spiritually.

How do you develop an interpreting ability? First of all, it's not given just to prophetic people — it's given to anybody who is willing to develop it. Leaders especially should develop the ability to interpret.

You develop the ability to interpret by: 1) recognizing its purpose for the church, 2) staying sensitive to the Holy Spirit, who enables you to discern spiritual things, and 3) being around other folks who flow in this gift, so you can see how it works and become secure with it.

It is amazing how many people don't know the personality of the Holy Spirit and His activities in the

New Testament church. That's why we have full-gospel, charismatic, Pentecostal, word-of-faith churches that don't know how to flow with the Holy Spirit at all.

He flows to the degree that we let Him. The Holy Spirit is a gentle Spirit. Even though He is strong and powerful, He is still gentle and respectful. He will never override what is not allowed. He won't do it. He will leave and go across the street and start with the church in the storefront. He will go somewhere else. If you want Him to stay, you have to let Him do what He wants and learn how to flow with it.

The church needs the combination of giftings and anointings of all its members to get to the place where it can receive the things God desires for it. You can't get there on your own. That's why the corporate anointing is so important.

Judging the Prophetic

But he that prophesieth speaketh unto men to edification, and exhortation, and comfort (1 Cor. 14:3).

The way you judge prophecy is by the three ingredients in this scripture. Is it edifying? Is it exhorting? Is it comforting? Even if it's a correctional word, is it still building up? Does it bring a security and an exhortation to live right, or a godly correction to something, so that the will of God can come forth in its mightiness and impact the lives of those involved?

Judge what I say by the Word. Judge what I prophesy by the Word. If it's not in line with the Word, get rid of it.

First Thessalonians 5:19-21 says: "Quench not the Spirit. Despise not prophesyings. Prove all things; hold fast that which is good."

How do you prove all things? How do you prove your inward witness? How do you prove the inward voice? How do you prove visions? How do you prove prophecy? By the Word.

Everything comes back to the Word of God. He will not speak anything into your life that is not already in His Word. Every leading you get, every prophecy you receive, every "knowing" you get — if it is prompted by the Holy Spirit — will line up with the Word.

The Word proves what is right and what is wrong. It is the ultimate judge. It is your plumb line for all things.

THIRTEEN

WAYS THAT GOD
DOES *NOT* LEAD

We've looked at the ways God leads His people — all the biblical forms of guidance, such as the inward witness, visions, prophecy and so forth. Now I want to devote a chapter to unscriptural forms of guidance so that you will not be tempted to try any of these.

The three main areas I want to warn you about are 1) fleecing, 2) a dependence on personal prophecy and 3) twisting Scripture to defend your sinful nature.

Modern-Day Gideons

Have you ever heard the phrase "putting out a fleece"? Well, be careful of it. In practical terms, "fleecing" is when a Christian uses some sort of physical manifestation to find out the will of God for his life. The trouble is, under the new covenant we are not to seek guidance by fleecing. God has provided a better way.

A lot of people have gotten into trouble by seeking spiritual guidance in this manner. I believe more folks operate by fleecing than by the inward prompting of the Spirit. That's because they are led more by their carnality than by their spirituality. They're more in tune to their senses than to their spirits and the Holy Spirit.

If you live out of the sense realm alone, you'll come up short in life. But if you live by the leading of the Holy Spirit, you'll have an abundant life.

Let's go to Judges 6 — which records the story of Gideon and his woolen fleece — and see how this whole business of fleecing got started.

When our story begins, Israel is oppressed by the Midianites, a pagan nation. The reason why God allowed this to happen is explained in Judges 6:1: "And the children of Israel did evil in the sight of the Lord: and the Lord delivered them into the hand of Midian seven years."

One day a young Israelite named Gideon was threshing wheat in the winepress "to hide it from the Midianites" (v.11). An angel appeared to him and said, "The Lord is with thee, thou mighty man of valour" (v.12).

Now, by natural human standards, Gideon was a coward. He hid his wheat in the winepress so that the Midianites wouldn't confiscate it. Later in the story Gideon "did as the Lord had said unto him" and offered a burnt offering to God, but "because he feared his father's household, and the men of the city...he could not do it by day [but rather] did it by night" (v.27).

So you see we have a very timid young man. He also had a poor self-image. He told the angel, "I am the least in my father's house" (v.15). Yet the angel of the Lord called him "thou mighty man of valour." That's encouraging, isn't it? Learn to see yourself as God sees you. He can do great and mighty things through you if you will just let Him.

During this supernatural encounter, the angel told Gideon, "Go in this thy might, and thou shalt save Israel from the hand of the Midianites: have not I sent thee?" (v.14).

God Himself, through an angelic messenger, commissioned Gideon. But still he required a sign.

> And Gideon said unto God, If thou wilt save Israel by mine hand, as thou hast said, Behold, I will put a fleece of wool in the floor; and if the dew be on the fleece only, and it be dry upon all the earth beside, then shall I know that thou wilt save Israel by mine hand, as thou hast said.
>
> And it was so: for he rose up early on the morrow, and thrust the fleece together, and wringed the dew out of the fleece, a bowl full of water. And Gideon said unto God, Let

not thine anger be hot against me (Judg. 6:36-39).

Did you notice that Gideon said, "If you will save Israel by my hand, *as you have said?*" Right there he should have stopped. If God said, then settle the issue. Why would Gideon say that? Why would Christians today say it? Because sometimes you can get to the place where you're tempting God. This is the only example in the entire Old Testament where God answered a person in this way. His grace covered the situation; God allowed for Gideon's timidity. But, especially in the new covenant, we should never tempt God in this manner.

Gideon must have known instinctively that God doesn't approve of this kind of testing:

> Let not thine anger be hot against me, and I will speak but this once: let me prove, I pray thee, but this once with the fleece; let it now be dry only upon the fleece, and upon all the ground let there be dew. And God did so that night: for it was dry upon the fleece only, and there was dew on all the ground (Judg. 6:39-40).

This is a wonderful testimony of God's love and His desire to help a man understand what is right and to be secure in that choice. But you have to remember that because of Calvary, some things are done differently in the New Testament from how they were done in the Old.

Because God sent His Son, we have a new and

better covenant that the book of Hebrews says has better promises and better ways. So there's something better to go with the better way. It's called the Holy Spirit in you. Don't get stuck in the not-as-good when you can have God's best. Go with what's better. The new and better way. Take the total benefit of what Calvary means to the church today.

Gideon placed the fleece out, and if there was dew on it in the morning but the ground around it was dry, it would mean God was answering yes. If the opposite happened, it would signify God's saying no. But God said yes. Then Gideon asked God to prove Himself again. This time, if the fleece was dry but the ground around it was wet with dew, it would mean God said no.

Once again God answered yes.

Many people operate like this today. They throw out fleeces such as, "If somebody gives me a word," "If this person calls me today" or "If there's a rainbow in the sky tomorrow morning."

We don't have actual wool lying out in our backyard, but we have all these contemporary fleeces. "If Brother Roberts comes up and talks to me at the book table, then I know God wants me to be a preacher."

Don't come up to me and tell me that because I shook your hand and said hi to you, you know you're called to preach. I shake hands with everybody I meet. Don't you blame me for your failure. My saying hi to you is not God; it's just being friendly.

Never make a decision on a fleece. So many people have made wrong decisions because of fleecing — even married the wrong person because of a fleece. Don't ever get married over a fleece; you'll get fleeced!

If you live by fleecing, you may be upset with what I'm declaring. But that's because you're so carnal that fleecing is the only way you believe God can talk to you. You're so stuck in your flesh and your traditions and your ruts that you can't hear God speaking to you and illuminating direction to you from the Word and from your spirit.

This might be the reason why I can teach some people how to be led by the Spirit of God, and they want to run back to fleecing because they're not sensitive.

They've not built a Word base in their spirits, and they're not praying to develop a sensitivity to the Holy Spirit. They want something they can see and feel. But it is rare that God does something this dramatic in the New Testament period of history. He doesn't lead people with fleeces.

Why? Because Jesus said to His disciples, "It is expedient for you that I go away: for if I go not away, the Comforter will not come unto you; but if I depart, I will send him unto you. He will guide you into all truth" (John 16:7,13).

Notice that word guide. The one thing Jesus said about the work of the Holy Spirit in the earth is that He will be a guide to you and me. The Word says He will guide you into *all* truth. That means all parts of your life, all types of decisions, all types of circumstances — the celebrations as well as the crises. He will be there to guide you and to be a help, not a hindrance.

Some people don't like the guidance of the Holy Spirit because they're full of rebellion and worldliness and carnality. And the Spirit's wooing and guidance brings conviction upon their carnality, and they override it. Pretty soon they aren't sensitive to the Spirit of God anymore. They lose all sense of His presence and shut out the sound of His voice speaking to their spirits.

When Jesus ascended into heaven, He said to the Holy Spirit, "Now it's your turn to go. It's your turn to operate in the earth. Holy Spirit, go!" And the Holy Spirit came as a rushing, mighty wind.

The Holy Spirit came upon all who would receive. Not just the priests and the prophets and the leaders of the church. He came upon everyone who would receive Him. Now we have that Spirit upon and within us. That's why we can get rid of all our fleeces and just go to His side and find out what He's saying and follow Him. Thank God we have a better way.

Prophetic Dependence

Thanks to Christ's work on Calvary, we no longer have to depend upon the prophet or prophetess to hear from God. We can hear Him for ourselves. I believe in the prophetic ministry with all my heart. God has restored it in a mighty way during this time in which we live. But there is a difference between the role of prophecy in the Old Testament and its role in the New Testament.

In the Old Testament men and women of God inquired of the prophet because they could not hear from God for themselves. They could not receive the Holy Spirit because He had not yet been sent for the operation of Comforter and Helper and Guide that He fulfilled in Acts 2.

Remember when Jehoshaphat said, "Isn't there a prophet we can inquire of?" And the people said, "There's one named Elisha who poured water on the hands of Elijah." And they said, "Bring him to us." And Elisha came, and they asked, "Tell us, what does the Lord say?" Elisha called for a minstrel. As the minstrel began to play, the Spirit of God moved, and Elisha said, "Thus saith the Lord." God then gave the word pertaining to the decision Jehoshaphat had to make (see 2 Chron. 18).

God wants to help us in our decisions. This remains a constant throughout the Old and the New Testament: God wants to be involved in every part of our lives, and He is never silent over decisions. He has something to say.

The problem arises when people depend on the prophet like they did in the Old Testment. In the Old Testament, prophetic dependency was correct. In the New Testament, it's incorrect.

The prophet's job in the New Testament is mainly the job of confirming what God has already spoken to you.

Now I will make a small allowance for when the prophet speaks things that have not yet been told you. But those things must be put in a place of judging and waiting until they begin to manifest. Then you can say, "Yes, the word of the Lord from the prophet was true" — and operate in it. But if you move totally by the prophetic word alone, you're going to get into trouble.

Every prophecy should be judged first by the Word. Does it line up with the Word and the character of God? If it doesn't find common ground in the Word,

run to where the common ground is. Be like Elijah —
gird yourself up and run. But if it is the word of the
Lord, say, "Yes, I receive it. Hallelujah. I receive it."

Another problem with the prophetic ministry today
is its wrong positioning in the church. A church that
receives every prophetic word without judging it
against the overall vision of God's work there is going
to have trouble.

You have to be careful that prophets don't become
the guides of the church, the ones you inquire of for
direction, because Jesus is still the head of the church,
and we have access to Him through the Holy Spirit
and through the Word. Churches that depend upon
the prophetic word alone become carnal, cliquish
and spooky in the long run because they leave the
Word and the fullness of the gospel and rely only on
that prophetic operation.

Every church has the ability to have the right prophetic flow in it. But never allow it to be the only or
even the main focus of the assembly. It can get to
where, pretty soon, the prophet controls the church. It
can also get to the place where the apostle controls
the church. These two are given to assist the church.

There's also more to the prophetic office than just
prophesying and giving personal words. In the New
Testament we see more prophetic preaching and prophetic praying than personal prophecy. Paul did more
prophetic preaching than personal prophesying.

What about the Scripture verse that says "Believe
his prophets, so shall ye prosper" (2 Chron. 20:20)?
Those are powerful words, but take them to the cross
for your specific situation.

It is right to believe a prophet who speaks correctly.

And, yes, you'll prosper. But sometimes this verse is used without giving you the right as a New Testament believer to judge it by your spirit and by the Word of God. Some prophets want you to take their words without any judgment, because they feel that judgment is an attack against them. That means they're insecure.

We all can hear from God for ourselves now. We don't have to go find the burning bush; we don't need to inquire of a prophet. We don't need to put out a fleece. We have the Word, and we have the Holy Spirit who is come by Jesus' command to guide us into all truth in our lives.

Prophecy sometimes is nothing more than just divine encouragement spoken by the Spirit of God through somebody. I used to watch people get all these encouraging words, and I asked, "What about me, Lord? I'm a preacher. I've given my life as a young man. I want a word. I have a right to get a word too."

The Lord said to me, "Why would you want Me to speak to you by somebody else when I can speak to you directly? I can speak out of My heavens, and you will hear Me down there in the earth."

That shut me up. You see, when you can hear God for yourself, you don't need somebody else to tell you something. But you have to build that; it's not a gift. That's why people want to inquire of the prophet and put out a fleece, because those things are carnal. They are easy to relate to, and they require no work in your spirit man. It's all done by the senses. But what I'm talking about is something you have to establish in your life — it's the main message of this book.

There are times when people are under assault, and

God sends somebody with a word. That word may be a Bible scripture. The person says, "Aw, I don't want a scripture verse; I want a word."

That is a word. And you probably would have found it yourself if you had been reading the Scriptures.

Twisting the Scriptures

The third area I want to warn you about is taking the Word and making it apply to your life out of God's will. If you try hard, you can find Bible verses for anything you want. Did you know that?

But if you're sensitive to the Holy Spirit, there are times when something inside your spirit just knows that a portion of Scripture has significance for your life right now. You know it's important to heed the truths that are written there — either to correct or to encourage or to adjust you.

Sometimes you can be reading the Bible, and something jumps out. You feel it come up in your spirit. Two or three days it'll keep coming. Hello? Anybody there? Anybody going to pick me up? I've been coming for three days. Open the door; let me in. I have something to say.

Find out what God is saying to you. Approach the Word eagerly, like a little kid whose been given a big piece of apple pie. It's set right in front of him, but he gets no benefit from the pie until he picks up his fork and eats. It's the same with the Word of God. All through the Bible we're told to eat the Word. Taste and see that it is good.

The Lord may give you just one word or phrase or

a person's name in the Bible or a time period in the Bible. Go into the Scriptures and search it out, because God is leading you to your answer or your correction or your encouragement in that story or in that part of the Bible.

But don't take a verse to defend your carnality, your incorrectness and your rebellion. If you want to, you can find a verse on why you should leave your spouse. You can find a verse on why you are justified in getting mad at your pastor. But unless that word is right — unless it lines up with what your spirit is saying — it's all just a dangerous game you're playing.

It comes down to this: Keep your heart pure. Cleave to honesty, not arrogance, because arrogance wants self-preservation. But when you're honest and you're pure and you want God and you don't care what it takes, He will speak into your life, and you will find your answer.

So, no fleecing; keep prophecy in the right place; and don't twist the Scriptures to defend your sinful nature. Let the Word conform you. Let the Word adjust you. Let the Word encourage you. Let the Word strengthen you. And, yes, it will defend you in the right season.

FOURTEEN

THE PRICE
OF OBEDIENCE

Toward the end of His earthly ministry, Jesus told His disciples the signs that would precede His second coming. He also had this to say about the end times:

> But as the days of Noah were, so shall also the coming of the Son of man be (Matt. 24:37).

What were the days of Noah like? The Bible paints a graphic picture for us.

And God saw that the wickedness of man was great in the earth, and that every imagination of the thoughts of his heart was only evil continually. The earth also was corrupt before God, and the earth was filled with violence. And God looked upon the earth, and, behold, it was corrupt; for all flesh had corrupted his way upon the earth (Gen. 6:5,11-12).

Evil thoughts, violence, corruption — sounds a lot like today, doesn't it? But that doesn't give Christians an excuse to sit back and wait for the rapture. We need to be doing what Noah did.

The Bible says Noah was "perfect in his generations" and "walked with God" (Gen. 6:9). When God gave a command, Noah obeyed (Gen. 6:22).

What God needs most in these last days is a church of obedience. God can use us fully if we give ourselves to Him fully. And that requires obedience.

Obedience carries a high price tag. It requires that you deny yourself daily. It requires that you crucify the lusts of the flesh. It demands your all for the kingdom of God. But its reward is eternal.

I have fought a good fight, I have finished my course, I have kept the faith: henceforth there is laid up for me a crown of righteousness, which the Lord, the righteous judge, shall give me at that day (2 Tim. 4:7-8).

And when the chief Shepherd shall appear, ye shall receive a crown of glory that fadeth not away (1 Pet. 5:4).

It's Time to Start Building

While Noah was waiting for the flood, he built an ark of safety. He kept on doing what God told him to do even as the people's taunts and jeers grew louder. Noah didn't have it easy, but he remained totally obedient to what God had shown him. He stayed busy right up until the day that God told him and his family to get into the boat.

Today God is declaring things to His church that pertain to the end times. We are to be building things for God that will last for all eternity — no matter what anyone else thinks or says about us.

When it comes to spiritual matters, the church will be mocked and taunted exactly as Noah was. So don't think it strange when people laugh at you and tell you you're a religious fanatic. To be used in these end times, you have to keep obeying and keep building your ark of safety. Then, when the storm comes, your ark will float.

Build According to the Designer

As I told you in chapter one, our ark of safety is life in the Spirit. By walking in the Spirit, we can fulfill our destinies in the midst of this evil day. We can be just and sincere toward our generation and walk blamelessly before God — no matter what is going on around us.

When the rains came and the waters hit Noah's ark, it floated above the flood all the way. Likewise, when the evil waves of the day come toward you, you will be able to float above all the garbage — if you have built your ark in the realm of the Spirit.

But remember: Noah built his ark as God described it to him. What if Noah had changed the design a bit? What if he had built a luxury liner instead of the ark of the Lord? Suppose he had wanted to take some friends along with him — against God's instructions.

The luxury liner would have sunk. A boat filled with ungodly friends would have sprung a leak. It is only the ark of God that will go through.

Some people like to build quick boats. They want to throw something together and "trust God" for it to work. But God does not work that way. That attitude is what has caused a lot of preachers, churches and ministries of the past to be covered up with the flood waters of their times.

They built a rubber raft or a prestigious luxury yacht instead of a strong, stable ark that could survive the storm. Your ark must be able to survive the forces of darkness and the pounding of the enemy.

Notice too that Noah *stayed in the ark* until God told him it was time to get out.

God has planned for us to stay in the ark *all the time*. The only time some people get into the Spirit is when they are in trouble. When there is a dramatic problem in their lives, they run to their prayer closets, where they have not been for months or even years.

Spirit life is not something you put on and take off like clothing. Nor is it living in a bubble away from the real world. Life in the Spirit is an everyday adventure that gives you the power, the protection and the authority to go to the corrupt world as Noah did and preach what God is saying to this generation.

The world desperately needs our message. It needs men and women who have built their ark of safety according to God's specifications. If you do not build it right — if your workmanship is shoddy — God cannot shut the door, and when the going gets rough, your ark will sink.

Let's stay in complete obedience to what God has called us to do. Let's build the ark of safety — life in the Spirit — and then we'll sail on into these last days, excited to be doing the works of God.

Passing the Test

Start checking in with the Holy Spirit inside your spirit. You have to do that as a conscious effort before it becomes a way of life. This is your assignment. Don't you love my class in the school of the Spirit? I don't make you write papers. I just give you an L for "Live it." And whether you pass the test or not depends on what you do after you turn the last page of this book and get back to living.

Will you be led by the Spirit? Will you practice your assignments? Will you earn your diploma from the school of the Spirit?

My sincere prayer is that you do. Don't settle for mediocrity. Get more of God in your life. Get out there where it's real. Walk in the Spirit.

For more information about
Roberts Liardon Ministries, write to:

Roberts Liardon Ministries
P.O. Box 30710
Laguna Hills, CA 92654
(714) 751-1700

If you enjoyed *School of the Spirit*, we would like to
recommend the following books:

Final Approach
by Roberts Liardon
Sometimes Christians get so caught up in debates about the end
times that they forget the real purpose for being here on earth.
That's the foundational truth behind *Final Approach*. It offers
readers a refreshing, positive guide to living in the end times.

Led by the Spirit
by Billy Joe Daugherty
The Holy Spirit gets involved in all the major decisions you
make. Author Billy Joe Daugherty uses his personal testimony
and practical principles from Scripture to demonstrate how you
can be led by the Spirit in all aspects of life.

The Dynamic Duo
by Rick Renner
With an in-depth yet easy-to-understand style, Rick Renner's
The Dynamic Duo offers a scriptural way to welcome the Holy
Spirit into your life. This hard-hitting message shows how the
Holy Spirit's responsibility to the Father is to help, teach, guide
and empower believers.

Available at your local Christian bookstore or from:

Creation House
600 Rinehart Road
Lake Mary, FL 32746
1-800-451-4598